Readi

The Tattoo

By Heather Morris

An Authortrek Reading Guide

Kevin Mahoney

Punked Books

First published in 2019 by Punked Books
An Authortrek imprint

www.authortrek.com/punked-books

First Edition

ISBN 978-1-908375-39-1

A catalogue record for this book is available from the British Library.

Foreword

Welcome to this reading guide to *The Tattooist of Auschwitz* by Heather Morris. My reviewing practice is to do a very close reading of the text, following in an author's footsteps. I write down my thoughts and feelings about what is happening in the novel as I go along, so that there is a record of my first impressions that is not overshadowed by what happens at the end.

There has been a mixed critical reception to *The Tattooist of Auschwitz*, most notably about its historical accuracy, and I debate the various issues in depth in this reading guide. In turn, I hope to spark even more debates amongst those who follow Lale's and Gita's momentous battle for survival.

Kevin Mahoney
March 2019

The Tattooist of Auschwitz page by page reading guide

Prologue

Pepan – this man was the main tattooist of Auschwitz prior to the arrival of Lale Sokolov. We see here that Lale looks to be acting as an assistant to Pepan.

"Looking up, Lale sees a man in a white coat" – this looks to be the first reference to Josef Mengele, the notorious Nazi doctor who selected patients for abhorrent experiments at Auschwitz. He was also one of those at the camp who selected which prisoners should be murdered in the gas chambers. However, we learn later in the novel that these events happened around about June 1942, so this isn't Mengele, who only arrived at Auschwitz in early 1943. According to Lawrence Rees in his 2005 book *Auschwitz: The Nazis, and the 'Final Solution'*, SS doctors had begun selecting which of the new prisoners were fit for work by July 1942, and sending those that they considered unfit for work to the gas chambers, so this scene fits in with the historical records.

"34902" – is what Lale inscribes on the terrified young woman. Lale tries to comfort her by smiling. Looking into her eyes, "his heart seems simultaneously to stop and begin beating for the first time". Heather Morris relates that Lale feels an instant attraction to this young woman, who is most likely going to be Gita, the love of his life. Obviously, Lale is not to know this yet, as the young woman soon disappears from the tattooing queue, with Pepan pushing Lale to process the next prisoner.

There has been a controversy over whether the Gita's prisoner number is correct. According to a *Daily Mail Australia* article by Lauren Ferri on 1st December 2018, "In the year since the book's release many have come forward saying Gita's serial number in the book is inaccurate, as women who entered the camp in 1942 were only given four-digit serial numbers". Ferri also relates that Gita gave recorded testimony for the USC Shoah Foundation, in which she stated her serial number was "4562". Despite the discrepancy in numbers, Gita confirmed in her oral testimony that it was Lale who tattooed her serial number. Heather Morris acknowledges the inconsistency with Gita's identification number later on in the book: Gita's son says she had the tattoo removed when she was in her sixties. Perhaps it is not too surprising that Lale appears to have misremembered Gita's number, as it was never her identity to him.

4

Although this discrepancy in Gita's identity number appears damning, I know from my own close reading of novels that there are always mistakes in long narratives such as this. For instance, in the first edition of her 2006 Orange Prize winning novel *On Beauty*, Zadie Smith mistakenly attributed a pivotal piece of art to the French Philosopher Jean Hyppolite, instead of the similarly named Haitian artist Hector Hippolyte. Heather Morris states that she thought Lale had told her that Gita's serial number was "34902". I know that as my years advance, and my hearing fades, I sometimes mishear names and numbers, so something similar may have happened in this instance. Heather Morris has stated that *The Tattooist of Auschwitz* is a fictionalised account of Lale's story, so it's rather inevitable that she will have made some factual errors while filling in the blanks.

Besides, as Heather Morris writes in the "Author's Note" at the end of the book, Lale had kept this story to himself for over 50 years by the time he told it to her, for "fear that he and Gita might be seen as collaborators of the Nazis". She goes on to write: "He told his story piecemeal, sometimes slowly, sometimes at bullet-pace and without clear connections between the many, many episodes." Given that Heather Morris was dealing with an oral account of events from so many decades ago, in fits and starts, I think she has done an excellent job of pulling all this material into a coherent narrative.

I'm reminded of another antipodean's holocaust novel, *Schlinder's Ark* (published as *Schlinder's List* in the US). Here are thoughts of Australian author Thomas Keneally in *The Guardian* on the 25th anniversary of *Schlinder's Ark* winning the Booker Prize:

> It was considered improbable that *Schindler's Ark* would win the Booker Prize of 1982. It was a work of faction, perhaps, in the Capote mode. It could be described as a documentary novel, but was it a real novel? I was so certain of the book's lack of a chance that I drank my nervous publisher's cognac at the end of the dinner in the splendid Guild Hall, certain there was no chance I would be called on to speak.

While *The Tattooist of Auschwitz* has been criticised for being not factual enough to be regarded as non-fiction, *Schlinder's Ark* Booker Prize win was controversial at the time, as the book was thought to be too factual in tone to win the prize for best novel.

Chapter 1: April 1942

Heather Morris goes back in time to present Lale in the cattle truck on his way to Auschwitz. She tells us that he was 24-years-old. However, the most commonly published date of birth for Lale Sokolov is 28th October 1916, which means that he would actually have been 25-years-old when he was on the cattle truck. In her January 2007 obituary for Lale, Heather Morris wrote that he was 90-years-old when he died in late 2006. It's possible that Heather Morris is not good with numbers, like a colleague that I've worked with that had a tendency to write the current year when recording birth dates, instead of the subject's actual birth year.

An Auschwitz cattle truck. Public domain image by Travel Buzz 2013

It's ironic that Lale is dressed to impress, as most readers will know that prisoners in Auschwitz will be forced to wear the iconic "striped pyjamas" that will rob all of them of any sartorial individuality.

"We stand is shit but let us not drown in it" – an elegant metaphor for the conditions in which the Slovakian prisoners are transported in, and for their predicament in general. As Lale will relate later on in this chapter, there are only two buckets in which the passengers can relieve themselves in. Despite the very cramped conditions in the cattle truck, the buckets full of slops would inevitable tip over, due to the staccato movement of the train. As Holocaust survivor Eva Kor has related via the website *Quora*, "There was one bucket in the corner. It had some sheets around it and I assume this is what was used for the toilet. But because we had very little to eat and drink in those four days, I did not need to use the facilities."

"Just remember, we are here to keep our families safe at home" – Lale tells Aron. Of course, unlike us, Lale is at this point unaware of Hitler's 'Final Solution'; his plan to exterminate Jews, along with the other minorities that he hated. Heather Morris then reiterates this point:

> Lale tries to keep his mind off theorising about what might lie ahead. He has been told he is being taken to work for the Germans, and that is what he is planning to do. He thinks of his family back home. *Safe*. He has made the sacrifice, has no regrets. He would make it again and again to keep his beloved family at home, together.

Lale's ability to deflate Aron's aggression may well help him and others in the cattle truck's final destination. Heather Morris tells us that Lale hopes to use his money and clothes to bribe "himself out from wherever they are headed or at the very least buy himself into a safe job". Lale still doesn't know where he is headed, but at the worst he suspects that hard labour will be involved, which he could bribe his way out of. Or at least Lale hopes that he can make use of his multilingual skills.

Those being taken to the death camps often resorted to using their possessions to afford some necessities, albeit to very little effect in Eva Kor's account:

> We would ask the guard by our cattle car for water. We were very, very thirsty. The guard would always say, "Five gold watches." The grown-ups gathered the gold watches and passed them through the barbed wire windows. The guard would take a bucket of water and throw it from the ground through the window. I put my cup over my head hoping to catch some water. The truth is I never got more than a few drops. I don't believe anyone else did either. As that was happening, I wondered to myself, Why are we asking for water and giving them gold watches, when the end result is we are not getting any water?... Today I understand why we were doing it. It was our only way of getting some information of where we were being taken.

"He takes them in, their brilliant colours flashing before his eyes, whole fields of poppies dancing in the breeze, a scarlet mass" - while on the cattle truck, Lale luxuriates in the beauty of nature, despite the poor weather. Of course, for many the red poppy symbolizes the bloodshed of the First World War, the 'War to end Wars', so while Lale may bask in their dazzling beauty

7

here, Heather Morris is doubtlessly using them to here to foreshadow the forthcoming slaughter of the cattle truck inhabitants. Lale seems not to have been caught up in the Second World War (which has been raging since 1939) until now. The phrase "he never knew that they grew wild in such numbers" is a bit awkward, for surely even the most urban of people most know that there are an abundance of wild flowers? Especially when you consider that Lale grew up in Krompachy, an area of outstanding natural beauty that is hardly urban. Then again, this paragraph could simply be a way of Lale having the chance to take the world in, to see things he had never seen or thought about prior to the oncoming calamity. It's a truism that time seems to slow down in the moments before a cataclysmic event. Again, Heather Morris emphasizes Lale's ignorance of the cattle truck passengers' fate – "When I get home..." Having written that, most readers will know even at this early stage of the book that Lale survives, and it could be that his positive outlook forms an integral part of his survival.

Heather Morris then relates that one of the cattle truck passengers dies in a fight. In Eva Kor's account of her own cattle truck journey, she knew that people in some of the other cattle trucks had died (presumably overcome by the heat and dehydration). Eva Kor thinks that someone may have died in her cattle truck too; it was just too packed with bodies for her to be entirely sure.

Lale relates that he is from Bratislava, a city in the Slovak Republic. Following the collapse of the Austro-Hungarian Empire in the wake of World War I, US President Woodrow Wilson wanted its inhabitants to decide their own future, which led to the creation of the First Czechoslovak Republic in 1918. Unfortunately the 1919 Treaty of Versailles was very punitive to Germany, especially with regards to the costly reparations that the German state was forced to make. Following that, Germany suffered financial hardship during the Great Depression of the 1930's, partly due to the ongoing reparations. Adolf Hitler's Nazi party thrived during this time of German economic hardship, and he became German Chancellor in 1933. Hitler had expansionist ambitions for the German state, and set about incorporating the German speaking inhabitants of the Czechoslovak Republic into Germany. These German speaking people lived in a border region that was called Sudetenland, and they comprised 24% of the population of the Czechoslovak Republic. The Sudetenland German-speaking population had not been consulted about joining the Czechoslovak Republic, and were poorly integrated in the state that was dominated by Czechs and Slovaks.

In 1933, Konrad Heinlein founded the Sudeten German Party, whose aims coalesced with those of Hitler's Nazi party. In 1935, the Sudeten German Party became the second largest party in the Czechoslovak Republic, as the majority of the Sudeten German population voted for it, while the Czech and Slovak vote was split into smaller parties. Following Germany's annexation of Austria in 1938, the Sudeten German Party made demands for autonomy supported by Hitler. Both Britain and France wanted to avoid another war, and believed that Hitler's ambitions were limited, and so they advised the Czechoslovak Republic to agree to Germany's demands in the notorious 1938 Munich Agreement. The Munich Agreement (British Prime Minister Neville Chamberlain's failed bid to appease Hitler) also led to parts of the county being apportioned to Poland and Hungary, and resulted in the end of the Czechoslovak Republic. Also in late 1938, anti-Semitic violence broke out in Germany during Kristallnacht, when the Nazi SA and civilians attacked Jews and Jewish businesses, supposedly in retaliation for the assassination of a German diplomat by a German born Polish Jew. This pogrom is considered by many historians to be the first part of the Holocaust, and Hitler's 'Final Solution'. (Then again, the Nazis first created anti-Jewish laws in 1933, as soon as they came into power.)

Following the Munich Agreement, the Slovak People's Party called for the autonomy of Slovakia, and the Catholic Priest Jozef Tiso became Prime Minister of the Slovak Autonomous Region. The following year, Tiso entered into negotiations with Germany to create a fully independent Slovakia, which was a plan supported by Hitler. Slovakia became an independent state under German protection: the Slovak Republic. In July 1940, at a conference in Salzburg between the Slovakian leaders and Germany, it was agreed that a Nationalist Socialist regime should be set up in the Slovak Republic. Tiso's preference had been for a Catholic state, but he went along with the setting up of the Nationalist Socialist (Nazi) regime. After all, Tiso had previously expressed anti-Semitic ideas throughout his journalism, so it was not a big leap for him to be party to the implementation of anti-Jewish legislation in the Slovak Republic.

All Jews were now required to wear the Star of David in the Slovak Republic, and were banned from public office, owning real estate, and taking part in cultural events etc. In February 1942, the Slovak Republic agreed to send 20,000 Jews to Nazi labour camps. The Germans accepted that the Jews would not be returned to the Slovak Republic, and the Slovak government paid Germany 500 Reichsmark for every deported Jew. The reason why the Slovak Republic government paid is that they wanted whole Jewish families to be deported, but the Nazis at this point only requested those Jews that were fit enough to carry out hard labour, so the payment would cover the costs of the unproductive members of each family for the Nazis. As Laurence Rees wrote in *Auschwitz: The Nazis and the 'Final Solution'* (2005): "The Slovaks... therefore paid the Germans to take their Jews away."

So, this is why Lale is on the cattle truck bound for Auschwitz. According to the Holocaust Education and Archive Research Team website (http://www.holocaustresearchproject.org/nazioccupation/slovakjews.html), "only a small proportion of the Slovak Jews were sent directly to the death camps." From this perspective, Lale is one of the unlucky ones. Then again, it may have helped his personal survival that he was one of the first Jews from the Slovak Republic to be sent to Auschwitz, as he may not have got the opportunity of becoming the tattooist if he had arrived later.

Hitler commented of Tiso that "It is interesting how this little Catholic priest Tiso is sending us the Jews!" Later in 1942, when news emerged that the deported Jews were being slaughtered in the death camps, the Vatican put pressure on the government of the Slovak Republic to stop the deportations. Despite earlier defiance, Jozef Tiso eventually agreed that the deportations should end in late 1942. As Tiso was still a Catholic priest, he could not ignore the pressure from the Vatican for long. (A peculiarity of the Slovak Republic was that many of its members of parliament were Catholic priests like Tiso.) Unfortunately, this stop in deportations proved to be just a temporary reprieve for the Jews of the Slovak Republic.

Pszczyna, the first town that Lale recognises as being Polish, is in between Ostrava and Krakow. However, we have a problem here, as Pszczyna wasn't on the route that Lale took, according to Wanda Witek-Malicka from the Auschwitz Memorial Research Centre in her article *Fact-checking The Tattooist of Auschwitz* in *Memoria* 14, November 2018:

> The transport could not have travelled between Ostrava and Pszczyna... Here she [Heather Morris] probably used the modern online search engine of rail connections which, a few years ago, due to the renovation of the Dziedzice-Oświęcim [Auschwitz] railway line, showed a significantly circuitous route... This error cannot otherwise be explained.

(https://view.joomag.com/memoria-en-no-14-11-2018/0766192001543510530/p6?short)

Bratislava (where Lale used to live) is only 40 miles away from Vienna, the capital of Austria. Of course, the Nazis annexed Austria in the 1938 Anschluss, so this means that Lale has been living very close to the Nazi Third Reich. Although, as previously written, the Slovak Republic government was a Nationalist Socialist regime that was very much allied to the Nazis, and a German protectorate.

Public domain image of Jozef Tiso.
Bundesarchiv, Bild 146-2010-0049 / o.Ang. / CC-BY-SA 3.0

Heather Morris relates that Lale spent a great deal of time thinking about his female friends in Bratislava while on the cattle truck. Earlier, Lale thought to himself: "When would be the next time he could give a girl flowers?" This already gives the impression that Lale is a bit of a "ladies' man".

Lale tells of an attempt to escape from the cattle trucks, by men trying to push down the wagons' wooden walls. Lale advises them that such attempts are fruitless, and again he is able to calm the situation. However, some Jewish prisoners did escape from the cattle trucks. For instance, in 1944 Lithuanian Kalman Perk managed to escape as there was a window in his cattle truck, from which one of the other prisoners had managed to remove barbed wire. Having been starved in a Jewish ghetto by the Nazis, the 14-year-old was able to fit through the window. In April 1943, there was a mass breakout from cattle trucks, although this was due to outside agency, as the Belgian resistance mounted an assault on the wagons in a successful bid to free some of the otherwise doomed occupants.

Heather Morris then relates how Lale came to be back in his home town of Krompachy – he had gone back as it became apparent that Jews around the country were being transported to work for the Germans. Lale helps his family now that Jews are no longer allowed to work or own businesses in the Slovak Republic. Lale's sister brings home a poster from the place where she is secretly working that demands that Jewish families hand over 18-year-olds and above to work for the Germans, or else the whole family would be sent to a concentration camp. Lale says that his older brother Max volunteered, but Lale took his place, as Max had a young family. Lale relates that when he goes to the local government office in Krompachy, he's processed by people he knew growing up, but does not say how he feels about this. The officials tell him to go on to Prague. It's not clear why the officials order him to go to Prague, as the Czech city was now in the German Protectorate of Bohemia and Moravia, and not part of the Slovak Republic. Although, Prague had obviously been part of Czechoslovakia before the war.

Heather Morris states that it took two days for the cattle truck to arrive at Auschwitz. Orders are being yelled in German, so it becomes obvious that this is their final destination. The prisoners are ordered to leave their possessions on the cattle truck – those that don't comply are beaten in punishment. Lale quickly realises that he will never see his suitcase again. He recognises that the German guards here are SS "Schutzstaffel", the paramilitary organisation known for their devotion to the Nazi cause and for their brutality. The SS running the concentration camps were the SS-TV ("Totenkopfverbände", i.e. "Death Heads", as "Totenkopf" is the German name for the skull and crossbones, used on German military uniforms since the nineteenth century. Lale sees that the SS are even using small boys as a labour force. I'm not sure who these boys are, as this is too early for the family camps at Auschwitz, and most children were executed on arrival at Auschwitz, as they were not able to do hard labour.

"Arbeit Macht Frei" – Lale is quick to recognize the cynical nature of the infamous Auschwitz slogan. The phrase originates from an 1873 novel by Lorenz Diefenbach, in which a gambler and fraudster finds redemption through labour. Diefenbach was associated with the Nineteenth Century German Nationalist movement, the main aim of which was the unification of

12

all German people into a single German state. (Prior to the 1871 unification of Germany, German people had lived under a variety of states). Obviously, the Nazis very much embraced the German Nationalist movement, which led to their using of this phrase. You can see the infamous Auschwitz gateway that confronts Lale below:

Public domain photograph, taken by Tomas Fogac in 2012

Auschwitz camp commandant Rudolf Höss copied this slogan from the gates of Dachau concentration camp. There's an apocryphal story that explains why the "B" in the sign is upside down: this was a supposedly rebellious act from the blacksmith that the SS ordered to make the sign, Jan Liwacz. (Auschwitz's first function as a concentration camp was to punish Polish political prisoners in 1940.) The Arbeit Macht Frei slogan was also used as a way of deceiving outsiders that the concentration camps were just labour camps (instead of being sites of mass murder).

"Just do as you're told, you'll be fine," Lale tells the similarly downcast Aron as they assess what is going on in this very alien environment. Lale tells himself to "always observe".

"Welcome to Auschwitz." Lale is astonished to hear these words from the camp commandant, Rudolf Höss, who then promises the prisoners that they will go free if they work hard. If they do not work hard, then there will be consequences. Of course, Höss is lying, as none of the prisoners will go free if they work hard. Unless, of course, he means that they will be freed from their hard labour by death. Höss tells them that they will be processed at Auschwitz, and then transferred to Auschwitz II – Birkenau. Birkenau was the Auschwitz camp where over a million Jews would be slaughtered.

When Lale is processed, he has to give his name, address, occupation, and parents' names. Then he is handed a slip of paper with a number on it – 32407. According to the Holocaust Education & Archive Research Team, "the prisoners were numbered consecutively so that we are able to reconstruct fairly clearly their order of succession and the fate which befell each separate convoy on arrival":

(http://www.holocaustresearchproject.org/othercamps/auschproto2.html)

There was a separate numbering system for women, which is why Gita has a lower number than Lale.

The green triangle on the uniform of those prisoners processing the new arrivals signifies that they were criminals. These are kapos, Auschwitz prisoners who were given administrative duties, or were assigned to supervise other prisoners. This enabled the camps to be more economical, as it meant that paid SS were not required to do all the jobs. The SS allowed these hardened criminals to beat and mistreat other prisoners. Indeed, it was an SS ploy at the camps to pit the prisoners against each other. Prisoners selected by the SS to be kapos had to be brutal to their subordinates, or else the SS would strip them of their authority, and they would have to go back to sharing sleeping quarters with their fellow inmates, who the SS would expect to murder their hated former kapo during the night. Prisoner on prisoner violence was very much a factor in Auschwitz from the beginning, for if one of the original Polish political prisoners stole from another prisoner's meagre food rations, then thief would be suffocated at night by their fellows.

Lale's shirt sleeve is yanked off as he is tattooed with his number. "How can someone do this to another human being?" Lale wonders. Of course, it will be Lale who will be doing the tattooing in the future. Lale thinks that he may be defined by this number for the rest of his life, as he is rapidly stripped of his individuality. According to the United States Holocaust Memorial Museum, the prisoners were tattooed so that the SS could identify their bodies after they had died/been murdered.

(https://encyclopedia.ushmm.org/content/en/article/tattoos-and-numbers-the-system-of-identifying-prisoners-at-auschwitz).

According to Auschwitz.org, the first prisoners to be tattooed at Auschwitz

14

were Soviet POWs.

(http://auschwitz.org/en/history/categories-of-prisoners/soviet-pows/).

Lale reveals that he slept in a school gymnasium in Prague for five days before embarking on his cattle truck journey to Auschwitz. Lale uses his language skills to translate the SS orders to his fellow prisoners. The SS tell the prisoners that they will get their clothes back after their shower. Lale realises that he will not see his clothes again, and while the SS officer is not looking, sets light to his clothes. The SS will not steal his money now, but "this might be the final act of his own free will". Lale comes to regret his actions almost immediately, as he realizes that such an act of defiance might have dire consequences. Fortunately, Lale is not pointed out as the arsonist. Even more fortunately, the showerheads turn out to contain just rank water. (Most readers will know that the majority of people slaughtered at Auschwitz were killed in gas chambers that had been made to look like shower rooms. The SS carried out this deception to ensure that the prisoners would be compliant with the gassing process, as the prisoners were made to believe that they were just having a simple shower before entering the camp.)

When they have finished their shower, the prisoners are given old Russian army uniforms to wear. These are left over from the 10,000 Soviet prisoners of war that had been sent to Auschwitz since October 1941, the same month that the construction of Auschwitz II Birkenau had begun. According to *Auschwitz: A History* by Sybille Steinbacher (2005), only 945 of these 10,000 Soviet prisoners were still alive by March 1942. Following their transfer to Birkenau, most of the remaining Soviet prisoners had succumbed to starvation or disease by May 1942. The Nazis hated the opposing ideology of Communism (which contributed to their appeal to those in the West who feared Communist uprisings such as the Russian Revolution), so the Soviets were yet another people that the Nazis slaughtered in mass numbers when they invaded Russia in 1941.

Lale is then dehumanized further by having his hair shaved off. There was a practical reason for this: to prevent infestations of lice that could carry typhus. The Nazis were not bothered about the prisoners getting lice, but did not want the SS to get typhus. Such was the war economy that the Nazis turned this discarded hair into products such fabrics. The Auschwitz resistance used typhus as a weapon against the SS, as they bred typhus infected lice, and rubbed them onto the uniforms of the SS. The wife of a particularly hated SS man, Gerhard Palitzsch, died from typhoid fever as a result of this germ warfare, according to Josef Garlinski in his 1975 book *Fighting Auschwitz*.

15

The wooden shoes that SS gave the prisoners at Auschwitz were every bit as bad as they sound, as they gave the prisoners blisters and pressure sores. These sores could get infected, leading to the deaths of many prisoners. They were obviously not suited for walking in through every mud as Lale does here. This is what Auschwitz survivor Primo Levi wrote about the wooden clogs in *If This is a Man* (1947): "Death begins with the shoes; for most of us, they show themselves to be instruments of torture, which after a few hours of marching cause painful sores which become fatally infected..." "...feet swell, and the more they swell, the more the friction with the wood... Then only the hospital is left: but to enter the hospital with a diagnosis of sore feet is extremely dangerous because it is well known... to the SS, that there is no cure for that complaint."

Those who struggle to walk in the mud are shot, the first killings Lale will witness at Auschwitz. Lale doesn't express any shock. Perhaps he is too exhausted and delirious to do so. Or maybe his initial reactions are forgotten by the older man who related this story to Heather Morris, given that he would see so much more death there. Starved and dehydrated from the train journey, Lale welcomes the rain and gulps at the raindrops.

The presence of the electrified fences signifies that the prisoners have now entered Auschwitz II - Birkenau.

Lale and Aron find themselves in Block 7. There aren't enough beds for the prisoners, and they are both too exhausted to fight for a place. Here's how Primo Levi described the sleeping conditions in the blocks in *If This is a Man*:

> [T]here are only one hundred and forty-eight bunks on three levels, fitting close to each other like the cells of a beehive, and divided by three corridors so as to utilize without wastage all the space in the room up to the roof. Here all the ordinary Häftlinge live, about two hundred to two hundred and fifty per hut. Consequently, there are two men in most of the bunks, which are portable planks of wood, each covered by a thin straw sack and two blankets.

Despite the violent deaths the prisoners have already witnessed, one of the prisoners can still joke about eating the paltry straw in the mattresses to quell their hunger.

Lale needs to go to the toilet during the night, and finds crude facilities at the back of the block. He sees some SS guards, so Lale holds back, and witnesses them casually executing three prisoners that were defecating. Lale is shocked to see that one of the SS guards is little more than a child. Now that the SS have gone, Lale takes the chance to relieve himself. He vows that he will leave Auschwitz a free man, and hopes that his family back at home are at least safe, and will be spared this fate.

Although Aron has already seen and heard prisoners being shot, Lale initially spares him the details of those killed in the latrine. Although when it becomes clear that Aron needs to urinate, Lale tells him to wait till morning, where presumably there will be safety in numbers.

Lale has a dream about the rich people that his father used to taxi around in his horse led carriage, such as Mr Sheinberg and his beautiful wife. Lale had wanted to grow up to be rich like Mr Sheinberg, not like his poor father. Such a fantasy of luxury seems to be a long way from Lale's current privations in Birkenau.

This is a recreation of a Birkenau block interior. Public domain image by Peter Tóth from Pixabay.

Chapter 2

When they are awoken the next morning, the prisoners instinctively choose safety in numbers as they leave the block. A prisoner accompanied by an SS guard calls out numbers, and the prisoners realize that he is calling out the numbers that have been tattooed on them. Two of the prisoners do not respond and are found to be dead inside (so presumably the three men executed in the latrines did not come from Block 7, or they may have already been removed from the list of prisoners).

The SS officer speaks in German, and multilingual prisoners like Lale translate for the benefit of their fellow prisoners. They will only get 2 meals a day, and the SS officer jokes that some of them may not live to eat the evening meal – although, if they follow the instructions of their kapo and work hard, then they will live. Their task is to assist with the construction of the hellhole that they have found themselves in, to enable the Nazis to send more unfortunates there. Some prisoners move to help those carrying their breakfast, but the SS officer tells them that they will be shot if they move. The kapo turns out to be Polish, probably one of the original prisoners. The 'breakfast' is a foul, unidentifiable liquid that Lale can only consume by pinching his nose to avoid its foul odour. Aron comments that Lale is "always so upbeat". This good humour in adverse surroundings may indeed help Lale survive.

The prisoners from Block 7 are ordered to help with the building of another block like their own. Lale is commanded to help with the roof. This job looks to be precarious, so one of the prisoners already working there advises him to observe at first. The prisoner who does this is Russian, one of the few left over from the Red Army prisoners. We learn that one of the many languages that Lale speaks is Russian. During their break time, the Russian advises Lale to stay on the roof, when he is less likely to be seen (and shot). The Russians' names are Andor and Boris. Andor shows Lale that the SS are rapidly expanding Birkenau to accommodate more prisoners, and Lale is horrified by the thought of how big the camp could become. Lale is cautious about talking in case he reveals too much, which is a policy that has also been adopted by Boris. Andor tells Lale that the prisoners with the green triangles – the kapos – are the worst, as they are sociopathic criminals. Prisoners with a red triangle are political prisoners opposed to Nazism, while those with black triangles are prisoners that have been labelled as lazy. The black triangles were also used to signify anyone the Nazis thought were asocial, such as lesbians, prostitutes, Aryans who had had intercourse with Jews, alcoholics, the homeless, disabled people, and those suffering from mental illness. And of course, the Jewish prisoners wear a yellow star.

Andor and Boris don't have coloured stars on their uniforms as they are prisoners of war (not that the SS afforded Soviet prisoners any of the POW protections under the Geneva Convention). Boris comments that: "They insult us by sharing our uniforms with the rest of you. They can't do much worse than that." Although, as previously written, 90% of the Soviet prisoners of war in Auschwitz in October 1941 were dead by March 1942, due to their harsh treatment there. Indeed, the hard conditions of Birkenau were originally intended for the Soviet POWs; the fact that so many of them had died by April 1942 meant that the Nazis could consider holding other prisoners there, mainly Jews. So this appears to be an historical inaccuracy on the part of Heather Morris. Either that, or Boris is utilising black humour when he says that this is the worst that the SS can do to them. However, there was a separate Prisoner of War camp called Auschwitz E715, which included British POWs, who were treated much better than the Red Army prisoners, as detailed by Duncan Little in his book *Allies in Auschwitz* (2009). These British POWs had privileges such as having a football team, but they could still be shot on the spot if they did not obey orders. Having written that, many of these British POWs have stayed silent about their experiences, as they believe that nobody wanted to hear about what paled in significance compared to the sufferings of most other Auschwitz inhabitants. Yet they were aware of what was going on at the camp, so their testimony is important as a counterweight to the lies of holocaust deniers.

During the evening, Lale observes other Jewish prisoners praying. He does not participate, and wonders what they are praying about. However, it's likely that the prisoners were trying to hold onto their identity, as well as having an urgent need to pray in such dire circumstances.

Lale decides to keep his head down, and to wisely never argue. Looking at the developing buildings, Lale decides that the "Germans lack any architectural intelligence". It is true that much of Auschwitz was built ad hoc, depending on the developing demands of who the Nazis wanted to be imprisoned there. Those in charge of the initial building of Birkenau were SS architect Fritz Ertl and construction Chief Karl Bischoff. Deprivation and cruelty were an integral part of the design: there was not enough water to supply a camp intended for 100,000 people, and inadequate means to dispose of waste. The SS deliberately overcrowded the blocks by putting in several hundred more prisoners than they were designed to hold.

Lale literally eavesdrops on gossiping SS, who consider camp commandant Rudolf Höss to be worthy of a black triangle (i.e. he's lazy), and grumble about having no access to beer and cigarettes in Birkenau. Lale believes that such knowledge could come in handy later. Lale is curious about the civilian workers who are not afraid of the SS. These civilian workers were Polish builders who carried out the more specialized construction work, such as the plumbing or electrics. Some of them did help the prisoners, although obviously the punishment for this could have been imprisonment at Auschwitz (i.e. death). Lale considers becoming a kapo, if only to find out more about what is happening at the camp, and what is planned for the future of prisoners like him. Although, as I was previously written, becoming a kapo was not a long term survival strategy in Auschwitz.

Lale begins to try to connect to his kapo. We learn that Lale can also speak Polish. It's not long before Lale accept the kapo's offer of becoming his dogsbody. Although the kapo is not as threatening as he first appears, it's apparent that he has access to meat from his foul breath.

Lale's curiosity is aroused by a truck. Now that he's a kapo's dogsbody, Lale seems to have a bit more freedom of movement. He sees that the truck stops next to an "odd bus". Naked men are led out of the truck and into the bus, which has been armoured with steel plates. The contents of a mysterious canister are dropped into the bus. It's not long before dead bodies are being carried out. This seems to be a curious mix of the mobile Nazi gas van, in which prisoners were herded into, and then secured, before carbon monoxide from the vehicle was pumped into the sealed chamber. The Nazis got the idea from the Soviet secret police, the NKVD, who used similar vans to execute people during Stalin's Great Purge from 1936 to 1938.

During a visit to Minsk in August 1941, the head of the SS, Heinrich Himmler, attended a mass shooting of Jews. Himmler reportedly vomited after witnessing this, and was told that the SS carrying out these killings were suffering from mental ill health from the stress of their savage acts. Himmler decided to find out if there were any other ways of carrying out such mass killings that would not affect those committing these crimes so much. Arthur Nebe was entrusted with devising new ways of killing. The first option, killing victims using high explosives, predictably resulted in the horrific outcome of human body bits being dispersed over a wide area that was very difficult to clear up. (Nobody could accuse the SS of being that intelligent if they thought this would be a good idea. Surely they had seen what happens when human bodies are submitted to mass explosives from the battlefield?) The SS also tried sealing their victims into a building, which they would then pump full of carbon monoxide, but this was seen as being too slow. So, they resorted to using the similar tactic of the mobile gas van, in which victims would be gassed while they were driven to pits to be buried in. It took about

20

20 minutes for the victims to die in the gas vans, and the van drivers could still hear the victims scream, which, like the mass shootings, affected their morale.

It was one of Commandant Rudolf Höss's deputies, Karl Fritzsch, who came up with the solution that would ultimately turn Auschwitz into a death factory. Auschwitz used a chemical called Zyklon B (a cyanide based pesticide) to delouse prisoner clothes. Fritzsch had some Russian POWs sealed up in the basement of Auschwitz Block 11 (where the SS tortured prisoners), and had the contents of some canisters of Zyklon B dropped into them in early autumn 1941. The SS didn't get the dosage quite right the first time around, as many prisoners were still alive, so had they had to use a stronger dose of Zyklon B to complete the slaughter. Like Himmler, Commandant Rudolf Höss thought that mass shootings were bad for morale, so he was very interested in Fritz's experiments.

Höss was told in April 1942 that Jews would form the main bulk of inmates at Auschwitz. Prior to this, the Nazis had decided at the Wannsee meeting on January 20th 1942, that all Jews would be worked to death in the concentration camps, and any that couldn't work would be immediately executed as part of the Final Solution. Höss had his men turn two cottages at Auschwitz – "Little Red House" and "Little White House" – into gas chambers. However, as their name would suggest, these gas chambers were too small to keep up with the influx of Jewish prisoners, as both combined could only hold 2000 prisoners at a time. So the use of the gas van would appear to be verification of the fact that the SS were struggling to keep up with all the executions that they were expected to carry out at Auschwitz. *What Lale appears to have uniquely witnessed (I can find no other accounts of it), is that the SS adapted at least one of the gas vans so that they could use it to administer Zyklon B to its inhabitants instead of the usual carbon monoxide.*

However, Wanda Witek-Malicka from the Auschwitz Memorial Research Centre is critical of this scene in her article for this very reason:

> The account of the murder of prisoners in a bus allegedly changed to a gas chamber does not find confirmation in any sources. This scene brings to mind movable gas chambers, but they were used in … Chelmno, not in Auschwitz. Furthermore, that statement that the SS men allegedly poured a poisonous liquid from a canister through a hole on the roof into the bus is simply false.

(https://view.joomag.com/memoria-en-no-14-11-

21

However, I'm inclined to believe Lale on this one, as it's such a startling scene, so I think that it's one that he actually witnessed. As written earlier, one of the reasons why I am forgiving of errors made by Heather Morris is that it is impossible to write such a long narrative without making mistakes, and Wanda Witek-Malicka is not immune to this. She writes that Lale had depicted a "liquid" being poured into the roof of the bus, whereas in Lale's actual account, the composition of the contents of the canister are not described (whether it's a liquid or a powder), just that the SS man "upends the canister". Wanda Witek-Malicka laments in her article that researchers from the Auschwitz Memorial Research Centre were not consulted during the publication of *The Tattooist of Auschwitz*, and I think that's probably a good thing, as that could have meant scenes such as this being removed from the narrative just because there was no other documentary evidence for them. What Witek-Malicka does not dispute is that "Ludovit Eisenberg" (as Lale's name is recorded in camp documents) was definitely at Auschwitz, and that he worked as one of the tattooists.

We know that the SS went to some lengths to destroy the documentary evidence of their mass murders when it became clear that the Red Army was near Auschwitz, so it's not surprising that any other documentary evidence does not exist for this episode. I think that the Auschwitz Memorial Research Centre do need to take some value from Lale's eyewitness account, and not to dismiss it entirely, as there are scenes such as this that add to the documentary knowledge of Auschwitz, rather than detract from it. As Wanda herself acknowledges, *The Tattooist of Auschwitz* is the only account written by an Auschwitz Tatowierer (which is valuable in itself), so the Auschwitz Memorial Research Centre doesn't have another narrative that they can really compare the book to.

I can understand why the Auschwitz Memorial Research Centre would be so defensive, as an Auschwitz account that is full of errors could possibly provide more reasons for holocaust deniers to attack the very existence of Auschwitz. Obviously, the work of those who deny the holocaust is, by its very nature, strewn with far more errors than are present in *The Tattooist of Auschwitz*. To holocaust deniers with regards this book, I would argue (using the words of Sean Connery from *The Untouchables* (1987)): "Who would claim to be *The Tattooist of Auschwitz* who was not?" Indeed, a reason why there are some errors in the book is because Lale delayed telling his story for 50 years for fear of being punished as a Nazi collaborator. One would have thought that at a time of rising anti-Semitism in Europe, the Auschwitz Memorial Research should be more appreciative of the global success of *The*

22

Tattooist of Auschwitz, as many readers will have gained far more awareness of the evils of the Final Solution through Heather Morris's retelling of Lale's story.

Some accounts of the transport of Slovak Jews that arrived in Auschwitz on the 29th April 1942, state that:

> The first of the Slovak Jews arrived at Auschwitz. They were taken to the two gas chambers and murdered. Their bodies were buried in giant pits. This was the start of the mass murders with which Auschwitz is associated – the deliberate and planned murder of, in this case, Slovak Jews.

(https://www.historylearningsite.co.uk/world-war-two/holocaust-index/auschwitz-birkenau/)

However, the SS didn't yet have the facilities to gas more than a couple of thousand prisoners in one go as yet. So the fitter Slovak Jews like Lale were not immediately gassed as the above accounts suggest, but were put to work enlarging the camp so that it could accommodate far more Jewish prisoners. We also know from later on in the book that some Slovakian Jews (such as Gita) arrived at Auschwitz weeks before Lale. The SS soon discovered that burying the bodies in large pits was problematic:

> At Auschwitz, the bodies were buried in fields. However, during the hot Polish summers, the bodies started to putrefy. Höss ordered that Jewish prisoners had to dig up the bodies that were then burned. Höss examined ways in which the bodies could be better burned after gassing. It was found that if they were layered with wood and other combustibles and placed on top of a large metal grate, so that you had bodies, wood, bodies, wood etc. in layers, they burned well.

(https://www.historylearningsite.co.uk/world-war-two/holocaust-index/auschwitz-birkenau/)

So, this led to the building of the infamous Crematoria at Auschwitz. However, even the Crematoria were not enough to dispose of the mass of bodies created when the Hungarian Jews were slaughtered at Auschwitz, so the SS had to resort to burning bodies in pits as above.

While the shooting of his fellow prisoners hasn't shocked Lale (presumably he has become accustomed to this during wartime), this gassing deeply shakes him.

Almost immediately, Lale falls ill and loses consciousness for seven days. When he wakes up, he finds himself being tended to by Pepan, the camp's tattooist. Pepan tells him that he has been suffering from typhus. Falling ill at Auschwitz usually meant a death sentence, because if the disease didn't kill you, then the SS would mark you down for execution for being ill. Indeed, Pepan says that the SS had put Lale into "a cart for the dead and dying", but a young man (presumably Aron) dragged Lale off the cart with Pepan's help. Lale learns that the men of Block 7 have been looking after him at night, while Pepan cares for him during the day. It's just as well that Lale never became a full kapo, or else his fellow prisoners might not have been so charitable towards him.

Pepan wears a red triangle, and says that he was too outspoken for his own good. He then reveals that he has been told that an increasing number of people will be sent to Auschwitz. Pepan offers Lale the job of working with him as a tattooist. Since there will be more people coming, more people are needed to tattoo the inmates. Lale is reluctant, as he sees the tattooing as a way of "defiling" people. Pepan believes that Lale would be a good tattooist, less likely to unnecessarily hurt his fellow inmates during the process. Pepan also argues that being a kapo's dogsbody could also be viewed as helping the Nazis. Lale asks why Pepan has chosen him, and Pepan says it was because a young man took the risk of trying to save his life.

When he goes back to Block 7, Lale notices that Aron is missing. His bed mates tell him that when the kapo asked where his dogsbody was, Aron lied to save him from being added to the death cart again. The kapo was so irritated at this, that he 'took' Aron, the implication being that Aron is now dead. His bed mates tell him that Aron wanted to save "the one", and then Lale completes this phrase that derives from the Jewish holy book the Talmud: "To save one is to save the world." As the Talmud puts it: "Whoever destroys a soul, it is considered as if he destroyed an entire world. And whoever saves a life, it is considered as if he saved an entire world." This quotation from the Talmud also featured in *Schlinder's List* for similar cultural and historical reasons. The men of Block 7 relate how they took turns to help Lale when he was ill, even exchanging his soiled clothes with those of a dead prisoner. Lale doesn't know how he'll ever be able to repay his fellow Jewish prisoners.

The next morning, Pepan takes Lale back to the main entrance of Birkenau, where all the dazed new arrivals are processed. This is probably just as well; otherwise Lale's kapo might have been vexed by his sudden resurrection.

The new arrivals to Auschwitz are all young men. "SS and dogs shepherd them like lambs to the slaughter", but this is certainly no Old Testament Jewish ritual sacrifice to appease God.

"Other new arrivals – the old, infirm, no skills identified – are walking dead." So even at this early stage in Auschwitz's role in the Final Solution, Lale knows that those who cannot work are doomed from the start.

Pepan seeks approval for Lale's employment as tattooist from Oberscharführer Josef Houstek, the cruel SS officer who was later given the job of running the Auschwitz Crematoria. It is precisely because of Houstek's cruelty that Pepan warns Lale not to be so flippant when this diabolical SS officer is around. Lale reveals that he can speak Slovakian, German, Russian, French, Hungarian and some Polish.

A Zyklon B gas canister. Public domain image by alanbatt from Pixabay.

Chapter 3: June 1942

Lale dreams about flirting with the women at his old workplace, which appears to be a department store. One woman in particular holds his attention, who had been followed to the main doors of the store by two Slovakian soldiers. Presumably this means that she was Jewish? She holds out her wrists to allow Lale to spray perfume on them, in an inversion of the role that Lale will now play of tattooing unwilling women and men. Lale's fantasy love affair takes in dinner, and then sleeping with the woman of his dream.

Lale is rudely awakened by gunfire, and goes out to join the rollcall. It looks like he's still sleeping in Block 7, but possibly his new status protects him from any ire that he might have received from his old kapo. Lale reveals that he's had affairs with several women, but that none of them have ever captured his heart.

Lale is shocked to see a queue of women waiting to have their tattoos redone, as he hadn't imagined that he would ever tattoo a woman. He also doesn't like the fact that the women are transferring from Auschwitz to the horrors of Birkenau (not that Auschwitz I was a pleasant place to be either). Pepan argues that if Lale doesn't do it, then someone else would and the SS would execute Lale. We then have a reprise of the book's Prologue.

Some weeks later, there is more upheaval as Pepan doesn't turn up for work. Oberscharführer Houstek informs Lale that he is now the main Tatowierer. Lale thinks that Pepan may have fallen foul of Houstek, who now assigns a young SS officer to watch over Lale. The SS officer immediately suggests that Lale moves out of Block 7 and into new quarters. Lale needs protection now that he works for the political wing of the SS. The suggestion is that Pepan might have been attacked by another prisoner in retaliation for working for the Nazis.

Lale suggests to the SS officer that the work will go faster if he has an assistant. The SS officer chooses the one prisoner that chooses to meet his gaze, and this is how Leon becomes Lale's assistant. Lale tells Leon that "the job" may save his life.

Lale finds out that the name of his SS guard is Baretski. *Historical spoiler Alert!* Stefan Baretski was a notorious SS guard, who unwittingly made headlines in later life when he was a defendant at the Frankfurt Auschwitz trials from 1963 to 1965. Baretski was born into a family with German heritage in Romania, although Baretski could never speak German that well. This is possibly why Houstek gave the job of looking after Lale to the misfit Baretski, as we know that Baretski could speak Polish fluently (one of Lale's many languages), according to the testimony at the Frankfurt trials by Polish electrician Henryk Porebski (*People in Auschwitz* by Hermann Langbein p. 419, (2004)).

Baretski was conscripted into the SS in 1941. Although Baretski expressed misgivings against the SS atrocities at Auschwitz, testified against his fellow defendants, and did help some prisoners by giving them water, it should not be a shock to any reader to learn that as an SS guard he also participated in the indiscriminate murder of Auschwitz prisoners. It was revealed at the trial that he devised a game called "Rabbit hunt" that involved ordering prisoners to remove their hats; the slowest prisoner to do so was beaten and shot "trying to escape". (Other SS men played similar games, as they got three days off every time they prevented "an escape".) Baretski was sentenced to life imprisonment plus eight years for the part that he played in the murder of 8000 people. (The 2014 German film *Labyrinth of Lies* is an excellent account of the hurdles the prosecutors had to go through to bring these war criminals to trial in a country that was still in denial about the many atrocities that that the preceding generation had committed during the war.)

Readers who want to know more about Stefan Baretski (and other SS men featured in *The Tattooist of Auschwitz*), should read the excellent book *People in Auschwitz* by Hermann Langbein (2004). Langbein was an Austrian political prisoner who was in Auschwitz from 1942 to 1945 (i.e., the same time as Lale). He was first imprisoned for having fought for the International Brigade in the Spanish Civil War.

The following is an extract from the Frankfurt Auschwitz trials:

> It has once again been mentioned that defendant Baretski, a *Volksdeutsche* (member of the Germanic ethnic group that lived abroad) from Romania, freely admitted that he recognized the extermination of the Jews to be unjust. If even this primitive defendant recognized the injustice of the extermination of the Jews, there can be no doubt that defendant Dr Capesius, who as an academic was essentially more intelligent and educated than defendant Baretski and is moreover married to a half-Jew, recognized that the orders regarding the mass extermination of innocent Jewish people was a universal crime-even if he was "only" a Volksdeutsche.

(*Beyond Justice* by Rebecca Wittmann, 2012)

Baretski orders Lale to take Leon to Block 7. Leon is effectively taking Lale's place in the block and as assistant to the Tatowierer. Lale tells Leon to tell the kapo that he works for the Tatowierer, although, as a new arrival, Leon won't know what a kapo is.

Baretski then takes Lale to part of Birkenau that is still being built. Lale now has a room all to himself. However, despite the overcrowded conditions in Block 7, Lale relates that he would miss his friends in Block 7 (not surprisingly, since they saved his life). Baretski tells Lale that he will now receive extra rations due to being the Tatowierer. Lale's new rations don't seem much better than what he was given before, but at least he is allowed to have more of it. Lale sees that his new dinner companions seem to fear and mistrust one another. Lale takes an extra chunk of bread and takes it to Block 7. He nods at Block 7's kapo, who surely must have realised some time ago that the resurrected Lale was no longer his to command. Lale gives Leon the bread as he knows that his protégé will have missed "dinner". Lale promises that now that he has extra rations, he will share it with the inhabitants of Block 7, although he wants to do this carefully to avoid strife within the block. Given that it's a high possibility that Pepan was murdered by a fellow prisoner for working with the SS, it's not a brilliant idea for Lale to visit Block 7 on his own now. (Although being assistant to the Tatowierer was apparently less problematic – it could be that other prisoners are resentful of Lale's increased rations, and may be aware that the Tatowierer has his own room.) Indeed, Lale believes that one of the prisoners called him a "collaborator" as he left Block 7, and fears that he will be accused of breaking the camp rules by another prisoner who's after his job and the extra rations that come with it. However, now that I've read the whole novel, I now realise that Lale's strategy of helping other prisoners may well have aided his survival at Auschwitz, and was certainly a better option than becoming a kapo that was expected to brutalise his fellow inmates.

Baretski takes Lale inside the SS Administration building, which, after the war, was converted into a church. Lale sees young women doing administration tasks. These women came from the SS Women's Auxiliary, the SS-Helferin. Some of these SS-Helferin worked as nurses also, but some worked as guards for female prisoners. (You may recall that Hanna Schmitz, from Bernhard Schlink's 1995 novel *The Reader*, was a female guard at Auschwitz.)

Lale asks for an extra table and tools, which are given without comment. So Lale believes that he has saved Leon from hard labour. The administration

28

clerk advises Lale to carry his tools bag at all times, and identify himself as "Politische Abteilung" to avoid any trouble. The "Political Department" was also called the "Concentration Camp Gestapo", so one could see why even the SS would not want to interfere with such a notorious departmental machine, of which Lale is but a minor cog. Indeed, Baretski warns Lale that he will be the first to come after him and kill him if he does anything wrong. (Now that I've read the whole book, I can see that Lale undoubtedly uses the fact that he works for the "Politische Abteilung" to his advantage, as there is no other way that he could have got into the women's camp later on to meet with Gita if he did not have the status of working for the Gestapo. Wanda Witek-Malicka in her article *Fact-checking The Tattooist of Auschwitz* criticises Heather Morris's account of Lale's ability to get into the women's camp. However, I would argue that since Lale was able to maintain a three year relationship with a female prisoner, he must have been able to get into the women's camp.)

Lale relates that incoming prisoners can arrive at Birkenau at any time of day or night. This especially makes Baretski irritable due to lack of sleep, and more likely to take this out on Lale and Leon. One night, Baretski is so tired that he can't be bothered to escort Lale and Leon back to their Birkenau blocks, and orders them both to report back at 8am. This causes a problem for Lale and Leon, as neither of them have any way of knowing what the time is, and obviously do not have any alarm clocks beyond the morning rollcall for Leon. So Leon volunteers to wake Lale up.

Lale and Leon both get up at sunrise. Lale tells us that there is a 4 kilometre walk between Birkenau and Auschwitz, although they may not be walking a direct route, as it's only about 3km as the crow flies. It's clear that Baretski has been drinking instead of getting much needed sleep. Baretski tells Lale and Leon that they must now walk back to Birkenau, as the transports have dropped the latest unfortunates there. Leon is tired and hungry, causing him to stumble. Baretski delights in tripping Leon up, seemingly to get a reaction from Lale, which is not satisfied.

Heather Morris writes: "On arriving back at Birkenau, Lale is surprised to see Houstek overseeing the selection of who will be sent to Lale and Leon to live another day". This is a possibly a sign that Houstek is now in charge of the Crematoria. Leon is so exhausted that he drops his tattooing stick when startled by the cry of a boy that he is inscribing. Baretski strikes Leon on the back with his rifle. Lale takes the risk of rebuking Baretski, saying that they will be able to process the prisoners much faster if he leaves Leon alone. Houstek sees the disturbance and intervenes on Lale's behalf. Baretski sourly releases Leon and tells Lale that he's lucky to be part of the Political

29

Department who answer directly to Berlin (and so are protected from the SS). Lale's rare ability to speak many languages has saved him from reprisal. Surprisingly, Baretski offers friendship to Lale, possibly out of sarcasm, but most likely because this will benefit the SS man in some way.

Unlike most prisoners, Lale knows the date, as it's written on the papers that Lale hands back to the Administration block at the end of every day. Lale reveals that Auschwitz prisoners were not required to work on Sundays. Of course, it's the Jewish tradition to have the Sabbath on the seventh day of the week (Saturday, if you count Sunday as the first weekday), but it's interesting that SS still allowed the prisoners to observe the Christian Sabbath on the first day of the week.

It's on a Sunday that Lale first sees Gita again with a group of other women prisoners. Despite the fact that all the women have shaved heads, and wear the same uniforms, Lale recognises her due to her very brown eyes. Gita also recognises him, and maintains eye contact, confirming that the connection that Lale felt on first meeting her was reciprocated. Baretski interrupts the spell, but is there long enough to observe Lale and Gita's mutual attraction.

Baretski offers to get Lale pen and paper so that he can write to Gita. However, Lale fears that Baretski intends to trap him, as any prisoner caught with pen and paper is executed. (Presumably Lale doesn't write on the paperwork he gets from the Administration block, and is only allowed to inscribe on human skin.)

Baretski takes Lale to Auschwitz I, saying that "Herr Doctor" needs more patients. Lale remembers the doctor with a white coat who held Gita's face with horror. As written previously, this SS doctor was not the infamous Mengele, as he only arrived in Auschwitz in early 1943. So Lale doesn't get Sunday off work.

Chapter 4

Baretski starts asking Lale about his previous life, which Lale uses as an opportunity to find out more about his SS guard. Although Heather Morris states that Baretski is only a year younger than Lale, Baretski was born in March 1919, while Lale's birthdate was October 1916, so the gap between them is more like 2.5 years. Baretski possibly lied about his age in this encounter to make him seem older. Lale's greater experience with women assists him here, as he is able to strike up a rapport with the immature Baretski by giving him advice about wooing women. When Lale points out that Baretski wouldn't want his sisters to be treated the way that the SS guard would, Baretski impulsively shoots his pistol in the air.

During the day, Baretski confirms that he was born in Romania, in a town near the border with Slovakia, and not far from where Lale grew up. (However, Hermann Langbein in his 2004 book *People in Auschwitz* put Baretski's home city down as Chernivtsi, which is 560km from Krompachy. Chernivtsi was part of the Kingdom of Romania at the time, but is now in Ukraine. It's notable that in the 1930 census, nearly 27% of this city's population was Jewish, and nearly 21% had German heritage.) Baretski's father physically abused his brothers and sisters. Baretski says he escaped by running away to Berlin, where he joined the Hitler Youth and then the SS.

Lale then takes up Baretski's offer of pen and paper, and tells him Gita's identity number. Lale reveals that he is still friends with his comrades in Block 7, even though he is working with the SS, and still shares his rations with them.

Lale wakes up and finds that Baretski is in his room. Baretski tells Lale that prisoner 34902 is in Block 29. Lale agonises over what he will write to her, but decides to keep it a brief account of who he is and where he comes from, who he trusts (it would be interesting to see if Baretski is on this list!), and asks her to meet him near the Administration block on Sunday. The moment Baretski has gone, Lale regrets putting 34902 in danger.

Baretski only gives Gita's reply to Lale after he and Leon have finished for the day. It's so late, that Leon has missed his evening "meal", and there are very few rations left for Lale. Heather Morris relates that Lale is now wearing the infamous striped pyjama uniform, which, unlike the Russian army uniform that he previously wore, doesn't have pockets in which he can store contraband food.

This 'striped pyjamas' uniform was worn by a Jehovah's Witness, and has pockets, unlike Lale's uniform. Public domain image by tiffffney from Pixabay.

Lale finally gets to read the letter from 34902, although he's frustrated to find that she hasn't signed off with her name. She writes that she is also from Slovakia, and arrived a bit earlier than him in March 1942. Indeed, 34902 was in the first mass transport of Jews to Auschwitz as part of the "Final Solution" following the January 1942 Wannsee meeting. 999 Slovakian

Jewish women were transported from Popgrad Slovakia to Auschwitz on 26th March 1942. She reveals that she works in one of the warehouses where the SS store the confiscated belongings of Auschwitz prisoners. These warehouses are nicknamed "Canada" because they contained a great deal of wealth that was inaccessible to the inmates, and because Canada was thought to be the richest country in the world at the time. As a woman who worked in one of the Canada warehouses, Gita's hair would not have been shaved (as Heather Morris depicted earlier), but long, as Laurence Rees writes in *Auschwitz: The Nazis and the 'Final Solution'* (2005):

> The majority of women in Auschwitz had their heads shaved, were malnourished and were easily susceptible to disease. By contrast, the women working in 'Canada' had access to food that they could take from the goods as they sorted them, and they were allowed to grow their hair. In addition, the SS mingled freely with the women who worked in 'Canada', not just to oversee their work but to pilfer goods for themselves.

The fact that Gita would have been better fed than most women in Auschwitz probably explains why Lale felt an instant attraction to her. Unfortunately for these Canada women, the SS that worked there were also attracted to them, and some of the women were raped.

Lale advises Baretski that he should quote poetry to women, but it's hardly a surprise when the SS guard says that he doesn't read books. Baretski says he has a girlfriend who loves wearing his uniform. Lale makes an outburst, pointing out that the girlfriend may only like the uniform, and not Baretski. Relieved that the SS guard doesn't shoot him for his petulance, Lale gives Baretski further advice about how to treat women, despite his repugnance this callow youth. Readers won't be surprised to learn that, according to Langbein, Baretski never married.

Chapter 5

Eager for his date with 34902, Lale is out of his room a bit too early for the hungover SS tower guards, who send a volley of shots in the direction of his room for their amusement. Lale rehearses what he will say to the woman whose name he does not yet know as he listens to the sounds of Birkenau waking up. Lale relates how the prisoners carrying the breakfast urns make more noise each day, as they become progressively too weak to bear their weight.

Lale plans to offer 34902 some of his rations. Heather Morris relates that it is nearly autumn in 1942. So focused is Lale on 34902 that he leaves his bag behind in his room and has to go back and fetch it.

Lale's encounter with 34902 is very brief. 34902 doesn't even say a word, but one of her friends tells Lale that her name is Gita.

"Gita" is an Indian name, as in the "Bhagavad Gita" ("Divine Song"). Obviously, Gita is not Indian – we learn later that her full name is Gisela, a Germanic name meaning "pledge" or "hostage". (Perhaps one could view her as a hostage in Auschwitz who will later pledge her love for Lale.) Readers will see that Lale is a nickname too, and that his Christian name was actually "Ludwig", a name of German origin that means "famous warrior". It probably isn't surprising that Lale and Gita favour their nicknames rather than the Germanic names that they were born with. Having written that, there's more than one "Gita Furman" in online genealogies, so it looks like Gita was a name adopted by East European Jewish families. "Lale" is a Latin name that means "to sing a lullaby", which is quite cute.

The *Daily Mail* Australia has reported that there is some controversy about the spelling of our hero's name: "Since then Mr Sokolov's wife [Lale's daughter-in-law] has found a piece of paper Lale wrote on and found that he spelt his name with an "i" instead of an "e" – and has allegedly accused the author of inaccuracies". "Lali" is usually a name given to girls, which could come from the Greek for "well-spoken". It also means "darling" on the Indian subcontinent. We don't know the context of the paper on which Lale wrote his name as "Lali". Perhaps it was a note to Gita, in which he lovingly changed his adopted name to the cuter "Lali"? For instance, I might sign off a note to my wife by spelling my first name "Kevvy". One presumes that Heather Morris spells our hero's name as "Lale" because this is how it sounded phonetically. Obviously, another alternative – "Lail" sounds phonetically identical to "Lale"; however, some newspapers (such as *The New York Times*) have taken to spelling our hero's name as "Lali". One would be interested to see how "Lale" is spelt in official documents. Surely Lale's son, Gary, would have picked up on any misspelling of his father's name when he first saw copies of the manuscript prior to publication?

(https://www.dailymail.co.uk/news/article-6448487/Controversy-Tattooist-Auschwitz-author-son-survivors-clash-mistakes.html)

(https://www.nytimes.com/2018/11/08/books/tattooist-of-auschwitz-heather-morris-facts.html)

We learn that Gita has two friends, Dana and Ivana. Exhilarated by her romance, Gita loses focus as she leaves Block 29 in the morning, and is struck in the back by the rifle of a SS guard, who is angry at seeing her look so happy. The SS guard orders that Gita and Dana not be given any food that day, and they are slapped in the face by their female kapo.

The next Sunday, Lale literally grabs an opportunity to speak to Gita away from the crowds. They each joke about how their day has been so far. Lale asks for Gita's surname, but she defensively states that "I'm just a number. You should know that. You gave it to me." Lale tells her his full name, Ludwig Eisenberg. However, Gita is more defeatist (or realistic) than him, and insists on just referring to herself as a number. Gita's omission of her name from her original letter was not accidental. Although one of her friends had said her name was "Gita" on their first rendezvous, this is just a nickname instead of her full name. Gita may have good reason for not revealing her full name, as she may fear that her family back home may face reprisals if she does anything wrong. (Langbein wrote that Baretski considered going into hiding instead of returning to Auschwitz while visiting Romania in 1943, but didn't as he feared the repercussions for his family.)

Gita tells Lale that the Germans throw the rotting food that the prisoners brought with them into the Canada along with the clothes, so that everything gets covered in mould. Lale says that he's heard some workers in the Canada have found jewels and money, but Gita hasn't found anything that she could use as currency. However, it was quite easy to steal items from the Canada warehouses, as Laurence Rees writes in *Auschwitz: The Nazis and the 'Final Solution'* (2005):

> The policy of the Auschwitz authorities – indeed, that of the SS throughout the Nazi state – was clear: all valuables taken from new arrivals were the property of the Reich. But while the theory may have been clear, the practice was very different. The temptations of 'Canada' were irresistible, both for the prisoners working there and

for the SS.

Lale says he will bring some food with him next time. Lale relates that he has definitely fallen for Gita, as seeing her smile makes his knees go weak.

Some of the personal items from new arrivals in the Canada warehouses. Public domain image by Waldo Miguez from Pixabay.

Chapter 6

Emboldened by his romance with Gita, Lale plucks up the courage to speak to the mysterious civilian workmen he's seen around the camp as winter approaches. They are working near some new brick buildings that don't look as though they've been built to house prisoners. Lale isn't really concerned about what the purpose of these buildings is, although many readers may suspect that this is one of the Crematoria that will soon be used to gas Auschwitz inmates.

The younger worker is hostile, but the older man is friendlier and introduces himself as Victor. The younger worker is his son Yuri. Both of them are paid workers from nearby villages. Victor says he's seen the plans for the building they are working on, and says it's called "Crematorium One". Now this is possibly a mistake on the part of Heather Morris, as Auschwitz's Crematorium One was built in mid-1940. It's more likely that the builders are working on "Crematorium Two", which went into operation in March 1943. Then again, the plans could be correct from the point of view that "Crematorium Two" was the first Crematorium to be built in Birkenau (Crematorium One was in Auschwitz).

Victor offers Lale a sausage, as he knows the prisoners are being starved, much to the ire of Yuri who may hold anti-Semitic views. Or possibly Yuri is frightened of being caught interacting with a Jew by the SS. Victor offers to come back tomorrow with more food. Lale asks for chocolate that he can give to Gita. As the encounter ends, snow begins to fall. Lale's face is full of tears as he walks away, presumably because he realizes that with the building of more Crematoria, the SS are preparing for more deaths as the camp expands. What he doesn't yet realize is the horror that lies in wait in the "shower" rooms of these Crematoria.

Lale cuts the sausage into small portions and heads in the direction of the nearest Canada warehouse. He finds two of the women who work in the Canada and asks them to smuggle out jewels and money, so that he can buy food for them and others. (This is another reason why Lale asked Victor for chocolate, which would have been even more of a luxury in wartime Poland, if he had something of value in exchange for it.) Due to all the confiscated goods from the prisoners in the Canada warehouses, there was a thriving black market in Auschwitz. Individual SS guards weren't supposed to help themselves to any money or jewels, but they did, as discipline within the SS ranks was so lax, as previously mentioned. The two Canada women agree to hide any loot they find in the snow behind their block. Lale gets them to swear that they won't tell anyone where they got the food from.

37

Lale goes to see Yuri and Victor. Yuri is much more pleasant to Lale now, as Victor says that his mother has had a word with him. Lale promises the two workers that he will pay them as they are taking a risk for him. Victor gives Lale two packages of food, that turn out to be sausage and chocolate. Lale worries about the consequences if the two women from the Canada warehouse are caught with contraband food. Despite the SS being prolific stealers of the wealth within the Canada warehouses themselves, they could severely punish prisoners caught doing the same, as Laurence Rees writes in *Auschwitz: the Nazis and the 'Final Solution'* (2005). Rees writes about the improbable relationship between prisoner Helena Citronova and SS officer Franz Wunsch:

> But whilst Wunsch looked kindly on her from that first meeting, initially Helena 'hated' him. She had learnt he might be violent: she heard rumours from other inmates of how he had killed a prisoner for dealing in contraband.

Likewise, Lale knows that he will be executed if he is caught with money and jewels that the SS have stolen from new arrivals. As Lale exchanges the jewels and money with Victor, he reveals that is New Year's Day 1943.

One of the Birkenau blocks. Public domain image by Peter Tóth from Pixabay.

Chapter 7

It's a Sunday, so Lale hangs around Block 29 in the midst of snow and mud. However, Dana tells Lale that Gita is sick. As we have seen with Lale earlier, sickness means death in Auschwitz, as the Block 29 kapo wants the SS to take Gita away and dispose of her in the death cart. Dana thinks that Gita has typhus. Lale believes that the only way to make her better is to get hold of some penicillin. However, I'm not sure that the SS in Auschwitz would have had access to penicillin in early 1943. As the *Encyclopaedia Britannica* states, in 1928 Sir Alexander Fleming discovered that:

> Colonies of the bacterium Staphylococcus aureus failed to grow in those areas of a culture that had been accidentally contaminated by the green mould Penicillium notatum. He isolated the mould, grew it in a fluid medium, and found that it produced a substance capable of killing many of the common bacteria that infect humans. Australian pathologist Howard Florey and British biochemist Ernst Boris Chain isolated and purified penicillin in the late 1930s, and by 1941 an injectable form of the drug was available for therapeutic use.

The ThoughtCo.com website elaborates further:

> By November 26, 1941, Andrew J. Moyer, the lab's expert on the nutrition of moulds, had succeeded, with the assistance of Dr Heatley, in increasing the yields of penicillin 10 times. In 1943, the required clinical trials were performed and penicillin was shown to be the most effective antibacterial agent to date. Penicillin production was quickly scaled up and available in quantity to treat Allied soldiers wounded on D-Day. As production was increased, the price dropped from nearly priceless in 1940, to $20 per dose in July 1943...

(https://www.thoughtco.com/history-of-penicillin-1992304)

Milton Wainwright, in his paper *Hitler's Penicillin*, states that it is perplexing that the Nazis were unable to mass produce penicillin:

> The fact that Germany failed to produce sufficient penicillin to meet its military requirements is one of the major enigmas of the Second World War. Although Germany lost many scientists through imprisonment and forced or voluntary emigration, those biochemists that remained should have been able to have achieved

the large-scale production of penicillin. After all, they had access to Fleming's original papers, and from 1940 the work of Florey and co-workers detailing how penicillin could be purified; in addition, with effort, they should have been able to obtain cultures of Fleming's penicillin-producing mould. There seems then to have been no overriding reason why the Germans and their Axis allies could not have produced large amounts of penicillin from early on in the War. They did produce some penicillin, but never in amounts remotely close to that produced by the Allies... One reason why the Germans were slow to develop penicillin was their longstanding commitment to the sulphonamides... The sulphonamides, however, often proved toxic, and bacteria readily developed resistance to them. Despite these limitations, the sulphonamides were effective antibacterial agents, making it seem to the Germans that there was no overriding need to replace them with penicillin...

(*Perspectives in Biology and Medicine*. Volume 47, Issue 2. Spring 2004.)

Just as there was greed and disorganisation within the SS ranks in Auschwitz, it's apparent that these factors were also at work within German industrial circles, preventing the mass production of penicillin. Milton Wainwright believes that the Allies' production of penicillin was a major contributory factor in the defeat of Nazi Germany, as penicillin saved the lives of many Allied soldiers.

So the antibacterial medicine that the SS had access to at Auschwitz was more likely to be one of the sulphonamides, than penicillin.

Dana and Lal are right to fear the Auschwitz hospital. As the Jewish Virtual Library relates:

The camp authorities designated Blocks 19, 20, 21 and 28 as the "camp infirmary" for sick prisoners. Prisoners often referred to them as waiting rooms for the crematoria. The lack of basic medicines and medical care caused many deaths... Throughout the period when the "infirmary" was in operation, SS physicians carried out various types of medical and pharmacological experiments that usually led to the death of prisoners or left them permanently injured.

(https://www.jewishvirtuallibrary.org/the-auschwitz-8220-hospital-8221)

Dana relates that she has lost all her family. Lale suggests that Dana and

40

Ivana should somehow manhandle Gita into the Canada during the day, and hide her amongst a nest of clothing; hydrating her while Lale attempts to get some medicine. Lale almost tells Dana that he loves Gita, but then asks Dana to say that he will take care of her instead.

Lale reveals that the death cart has been named "Black Mary".

Lale goes to Victor the next day to ask if he can hold of a medicine like penicillin, although it's even less likely that a Polish construction worker would have means to access penicillin than the SS, unless purloined from one of the Crematoria.

Lale is relieved to see that Dana and Ivana are managing to hold up Gita on the way to the Canada. Lale is startled by Baretski appearing behind him, asking him why he's there. Lale says that he'd been feeling sick that morning, so Baretski offers to take him to the 'hospital'. Lale replies that he'd rather that Baretski shoot him than send him there. Baretski withdraws his gun from his holster as if to oblige, but Lale reminds Baretski that they have work to do. Baretski tells Lale to return his blanket back to his quarters (Lale presumably took the blanket with him to keep warm in the freezing cold).

So anxious is Lale about Gita that he accidentally presses too hard while doing the tattoos of some prisoners. He rushes back to Block 29 with all his breakfast rations. Dana says that they have been able to keep Gita safe during the day. The next day, Victor puts the medicine into Lale's tattooing bag (very handy for Lale to have this for smuggling goods), and Lale is able to take it to Gita.

Fortunately, Victor has managed to get a liquid medicine that Gita is able to take, although Dana and Ivana have doubts that Gita will recover. Lale is relieved to see that Gita is still alive in the morning, and appears a bit more alert when Dana and Ivana transport her to the Canada.

Lale then goes in search of Baretski to ask him a favour. Baretski initially refuses, but Lale argues that he might be able to return the favour one day. Lale asks Baretski if he can get Gita to be transferred from the Canada to the Administration building, where it's warmer. While it might have been warmer in the Administration block, Laurence Rees writes in *Auschwitz: The Nazis and the 'Final Solution'* (2005): "It is not surprising that proportionately more women survived Auschwitz as a result of working in 'Canada' than almost anywhere else." This is because the SS in Canada would work with the same women every day, and got to see the prisoners as human beings that they were less likely to kill or harm on a whim.

Lale is able to meet up with the recovering Gita the following Sunday. She's wearing a long overcoat from the Canada that the SS have not objected to. Lale doesn't dare touch Gita in case one of the SS takes objection to their fraternisation.

Gita fears the worst when she's taken to the Administration building, weak as she still is from the typhus. She soon notices that the building has heating on, as the SS work there along with female civilians and female prisoners. Gita is put to work, updating records. There is still danger there, as her colleague implicitly warns her to stay silent. However, she can't help but exclaim when she sees Lale visiting the Administration building later that day, as part of his duties. So, Lale has not only found a way to keep Gita warm, but also provide more opportunity of seeing her.

Gita makes friends with her colleague, who is called Cilka, from Block 25. This may be another error in the novel, as Block 25, the so-called "Death Block", was not a great block to be in:

> If the gas chambers were occupied, the condemned prisoners were placed in barrack 25 (called the "death block" by the prisoners, which stood apart from the rest of the camp... Sobs and groans of women awaiting death could be heard from there; they pushed their hands through the bars, begging for water. Descriptions of block 25 and the process of removing the Jewish women prisoners to the gas chamber are found in numerous memoirs of former prisoners.

(*Anatomy of the Auschwitz Death Camp* by Yisrael Gutman and Michael Berenbaum, 1994)

Although Lale is waiting for Gita at the end of the day, he can't approach her due to so many SS hanging around. Gita takes Cilka to meet her friends in Block 29. Gita fears that Dana and Ivana might be jealous about her new work, but they are just relieved that she is safe. All three are amazed when they see that Cilka has a full head of hair when she removes her headscarf (although one suspects that there may be a price to be paid for such a privilege). Gita runs her hand through the stubble on her head that she knows will be shaved soon. For some reason, Cilka now appears to move into Block 29; obviously, this is a much safer block than 25 (if she was ever in 25), but some strings must have been pulled for Cilka to move blocks. Or this is possibly dramatic licence on the part of Heather Morris.

Chapter 8

The fact that Italian Jews are now being processed at Auschwitz is an indication that time has marched on, as before Italy surrendered to the Allies on 8th September 1943, life had been relatively safe for Jews in Italy. This was much to the frustration of Nazi Germany, as they believed the refusal of Mussolini's regime to hand over their Jews encouraged other Axis powers to refuse to do so also. Following the Italian surrender, the Nazis occupied Italy and began to export Italian Jews (and the Jews that had fled to Italy) to concentration camps.

The Norwegian Jews had been transported to Auschwitz much earlier, in November 1942, with another transport that arrived in March 1943.

Heather Morris relates that those incoming prisoners who have been selected for death by the medical team are tattooed at Auschwitz I, while those selected for work are transported by train to Birkenau to be processed and tattooed. Lale and Leon are only doing the Birkenau tattooing, so this saves them both an 8 kilometre round walk.

With so many new arrivals to process, Lale has been unable to get over to the Canada warehouse to collect the money and jewels, or meet up with Victor. Lale does apparently make it over to the warehouse more often, as Heather Morris says that money and jewellery are piling up in his room. Lale is so tired from tattooing all the new arrivals on this day that he drops the arm of the man he has been tattooing. Lale takes the risk of asking this giant of a man what his name is after he whispers that he's very hungry. The giant says that his name is Jakub.

Lale must do the tattooing in the open air, as he asks Jakub to hide in the shadows, out of the floodlights. Taking a great many risks, Lale takes Jakub back to his room and gives him some of the food from Victor. Jakub reveals that he's from America, and was visiting his family in Poland, when he was rounded up and sent to Auschwitz.

Lale says that, due to Jakub's obvious physical strength, the SS will probably want to keep him alive, as he will be able to do physical labour that others cannot. Fortunately Jakub already knows what block he has been assigned to (Block 7), so Lale is able to sneak him there before anyone notices that he is missing. Having a friend with such physical strength may prove handy to Lale.

Two days later, it is Sunday. Lale relates that he has been so busy processing newcomers that he hasn't been able to see Gita for five Sundays. (So maybe Lale doesn't see her so often at the Administration block.)

Jakub has become the centre of attention by showing off his strength. Unfortunately, this attracts the SS also. Under the direction of Houstek, the SS take Jakub away for some reason.

Lale sees Gita and takes her to their spot behind the Administration building. Heather Morris states that the ground is still too cold for Gita to sit on, which suggests that this may still be the end of winter in early 1943, and not autumn 1943, which was suggested by her earlier mention of Italian Jewish prisoners at Auschwitz. The two delight in feeding each other contraband chocolate. They kiss each other passionately (perhaps they no longer fear the SS taking exception to this?). Lale offers her one of his purloined diamond rings, but Gita decides not to take it in the end (as possibly this is a bit too risky).

Lale and Gita hold hands as they go back to the compound, but quickly release them when they see Baretski.

Baretski tells Lale that they have work to do at Auschwitz I. For some reason, Baretski is very tense and doesn't even acknowledge his fellow SS guards when they call out to him. They come across three workers who have fallen on the ground, exhausted. Baretski executes them without a second thought.

In the Frankfurt Auschwitz trial, Baretski revealed how young SS men were shown anti-Jewish Nazi films at the camp:

> "In those days we were shown rabble rousing films like *Jud Süß* and *Ohm Krüger*. I remember these two titles! The films were screened for the SS staff – and how the inmates looked the next day!" Erich Kolhagen remembers that he and other Jews in the penal colony at Sachsenhausen were beaten up after the SS had watched the film *Jud Süß* the evening before.

(*People in Auschwitz* by Hermann Langbein, 2004)

Possibly Baretski had been watching *Jud Süß* the night before. Or he commits these murders just because he is in a foul mood. Such were the risks of being an inmate at Auschwitz.

Chapter 9: March 1943

Heather Morris provides with the date, and it becomes clear that her mention of Italian Jewish arrivals was a bit too early at the start of the previous chapter. Lale reports to the Administration building to get his instructions, and winks at Gita and Cilka. Lale is given his instructions by a Polish woman, Bella.

Lale asks Bella why each of the numbers is to have a "Z" in front, but Bella doesn't know. The SS gave Romany prisoners in Auschwitz identity numbers that began with a "Z". The first transport of Romany people to Auschwitz occurred on 26th February 1943, according to Auschwitz.org.

(http://auschwitz.org/en/museum/auschwitz-prisoners/prisoner-numbers).

Bella seems to arrange a brief romantic encounter between Lale and Gita.

Lale and Leon are shocked to see children amongst the new arrivals. According to Auschwitz.org:

> On December 16, 1942, Heinrich Himmler ordered the deportation of all remaining Sinti and Roma to a concentration camp. The implementing regulations for this order, issued by the RSHA on January 29, 1943, specified that Auschwitz was the place of deportation. As a result of this ruling, the Gypsy family camp known as the Zigeunerlager (Gypsy camp), which existed for 17 months, was set up in Auschwitz-Birkenau sector BIIe... It is estimated that about 23 thousand men, women, and children were imprisoned in the camp.

(http://auschwitz.org/en/history/categories-of-prisoners/sinti-and-roma-gypsies-in-auschwitz/).

According to the Holocaust Memorial Day Trust website:

> Unlike the Jews, Roma men, women and children were not separated, which is why the camp was called Zigeunerfamilienlager (Gypsy Family Camp). There was no selection to divide those fit for work and those immediately destined for the gas chambers either, and very few were conscripted to do forced labour outside the Zigeunerfamilienlager, although some had to work in the camp itself. All arrivals were tattooed on their arms (babies on their thighs) with a number prefixed by a Z for Zigeuner, meaning

45

Gypsy. Their hair was shorn off, but they were allowed to grow it again. Most kept their clothing, but they had to wear a black triangle (for 'asocial') attached to it…

(https://www.hmd.org.uk/news/auschwitz-birkenaus-gypsy-family-camp/)

Leon is reluctant to tattoo children, but Baretski is clear in his instructions that they are to inscribe all the new arrivals that hand them a number. Baretski is even more disdainful about the new arrivals than he is about Jews. However, contrary to the Holocaust Memorial Day Trust website quotation above, Lale and Leon find that they do not have to tattoo the children, "though some presenting numbers seem too young to Lale". Possibly these younger ones wanting to be tattooed are doing this to be spared death. It's highly likely that if Lale and Leon had refused to tattoo children, then they would have been summarily executed. Or possibly that Lale did not want to admit to tattooing children, as tattooing adults is one thing, but to tattoo innocent children… It's likely that Lale did not want to be seen as being complicit in the abuse of children, as children at Auschwitz were tattooed. As Heather Morris acknowledged earlier, when she wrote that some prisoners were being tattooed in Auschwitz I, while Lale and Leon did the tattooing at Birkenau, Lale and Leon were not the only tattooists at Auschwitz, and so someone else may have tattooed the children. Or perhaps Lale and Leon tattooed the children later in a scene that is not depicted in the novel.

The Romany and Sinti were yet another group of people that the Nazis thought were inferior. According to Auschwitz.org:

The Nazi Germans regarded Sinti and Roma… as enemies of the Third Reich, and therefore sentenced them to isolation and extermination. Nazi Germany followed pseudoscientific arguments supplied by the Institute for the Study of Racial Hygiene and established strict principles for dealing with the Sinti and Roma, whom it regarded as racially alien, inferior, and "asocial". In the first years after they came to power, the Nazis introduced a range of anti-Gypsy restrictions, including an obligation for them to register and submit to "racial examination"…

(http://auschwitz.org/en/history/categories-of-prisoners/sinti-and-roma-gypsies-in-auschwitz/).

I had a feeling that there would be a terrible price to be paid for Cilka keeping her hair, and so it proves as she is dragged off to a room with a bed, in which Lagerfuhrer Johann Schwarzhuber, senior Commandant of

Birkenau, is present. Schwarzhuber proceeds to rape her.

Women were indeed at great risk of sexual violence in Auschwitz. For instance, Laurence Rees in *Auschwitz: the Nazis and the 'Final Solution'* (2005) writes that the SS had showers installed behind a Canada warehouse which women prisoners could use:

> "Once, a girl from Bratislava was taking a shower. She was a pretty woman, not skinny. An SS officer came to her and misused her in the shower – he raped her." The SS man responsible was subsequently transferred out of 'Canada' but escaped further punishment.

It should be noted here that the SS man was not punished for the rape itself, but for having sexual relations with a Jewish woman. So although Gita no longer works in the Canada warehouse, she is still at risk of suffering the sexual violence inflicted on Cilka.

Cilka is obviously not returned to the Administration block, as Gita goes back to her block distraught without Cilka.

When he goes back to his block that night, Lale finds children playing tag, and that the bunk beds in his previously empty blocked are being filled. Lale finds that he can talk to the children using a variant of Hungarian. He tells the children never to enter his room, but is unsure if they will obey him. Lale might share the common prejudices against the Romany as he considers if the contraband in his room is now safe. Lale reveals that he is in the room in the block that is usually reserved for a kapo.

The Romany ask Lale what will happen to them – Lale doesn't know, but he makes good relations with them. Lale has to adapt to sleeping in a noisier environment.

Chapter 10

So good are Lale's relations with these newcomers, he becomes an "honorary Romany". It becomes clear that Lale is now living in the "Gypsy Camp", the Zigeunerfamilienlager. *Historical Spoiler Alert!* Those who know their Auschwitz history will know that this is not a particularly good place to be, and that its inhabitants are doomed for the most part. (It is much like everywhere else in Auschwitz then.) The children know that he has access to food, and Lale gives them what he can, but explains that he will give food to the adults to portion out.

Lale's suggestion that they school the children gives the older women a new lease of life, as they tell the children stories from Romany culture. Lale is intrigued by the Romany nomadic way of life.

Lale becomes friendly with one older woman who has no family of her own, (Nadya) as her husband and son succumbed to typhus. Nadya reminds Lale of his absent mother, and he begins to wonder what will become of his family back home.

Indeed, as he arrives back in the block one night, a small boy reminds him of his brother's son. Lale remembers the last time he saw his family, at the train station as he left to go to Prague over a year ago. He remembers being surprised at seeing tears in his father's eyes, and his mother with her arms outstretched towards him. Obviously, one thinks there is always the risk that he would see his family in even more wretched circumstances: in Auschwitz.

Lale puts his troubles behind him as he plays with the Zigeunerfamilienlager children. He then talks to the men, and they each joke that in another life they would have crossed the road to avoid each other; these seem petty prejudices compared with the monstrosity of the 'Final Solution' that has made them see common ground.

Nadya joins Lale briefly. Nadya's hair has not been shaved. Lale observes that she has a very quiet, emotionless voice. She tells Lale that "Nadya" means "hope". "Nadya" is indeed a Russian name that means "hope". However, there is very little of that in Auschwitz.

Chapter 11: May 1943

Lale and Leon are tattooing some incoming female prisoners. There appears to be a new doctor in a white coat making 'selections'. This doctor is a bit different, as he's whistling the tune from an opera. Leon turns pale at the sight of him, and Lale is disturbed. Even Baretski says *"I'm* scared of him. This guy's a creep." As Robert Jay Lifton writes in his 1985 *New York Times* article *What Made This Man? Mengele,* unlike the other doctors, Mengele seemed to enjoy the selections, and whistled while he was doing it. Baretski confirms that the doctor is Josef Mengele, who is looking for "particular patients". Lale is aware that being sick is not a criterion for such selections.

Later that morning, Lale is so startled by Mengele's whistling, that his tattooing pen slips, causing a woman to bleed. Mengele seems to enjoy spooking the Tatowierer.

Lale can't help watching Mengele at work, for he can't see any logic to Mengele's selections, as Mengele sends apparently healthy young women to their deaths. Mengele is aware of the challenging way that Lale is staring at him, and sends an SS officer over, who takes Leon away despite Lale's protestations that they have so much work to do. Obviously, Lale is pleading for Leon's life here. Leon interjects, to prevent Lale from challenging the SS any more, and is led away.

Lale walks back to Birkenau alone that night. He sees a "blood red" poppy, which Heather Morris probably intends as an ominous metaphor for Leon's fate. Of course, Lale also saw poppies on his fateful transport to Auschwitz, and thought of women then too. He wonders if his mother will ever get to meet Gita, and if they will get along. Of course, this is something that he imagines occurring outside the confines of Auschwitz, as he would never wish for his mother to be there. As written earlier, it's entirely possible that the rest of Lale's family would be sent to Auschwitz.

There follows a bit of an odd passage in which Heather Morris relates that Lale learnt how to get on with women by flirting with his mother. Morris says that Lale's friends reacted with shock when he told them about this, but when he asked them about their relations with their own mothers, Lale could see evidence that they flirted with their mothers. His friends put this down to their mothers being more easily persuadable when they wanted things. This sounds a bit too much like Sigmund Freud's Oedipus Complex to me, in which a child has an unconscious sexual desire for the opposite sex parent, and a hatred of the same sex parent. Freud named his concept after the ancient Greek tragic hero who unwittingly killed his father and married his mother. Not that there was an unconscious sexual desire on Oedipus's part; he simply didn't know his parents, as he was cast out when he was born, due to a prophecy which said that he would kill his father. Obviously, Lale doesn't subconsciously hate his father, as per Freud. However, Lale's belief that he learnt all about women from flirting with his mother sounds just as outlandish as Freud's theory, especially to those men whose mothers didn't form as close as an attachment to them as Lale's mother did to him.

Lale picks up the poppy to give to Gita the next day, but when he awakes, he finds that it has disintegrated and become an even greater symbol of death.

This replica of the bunk beds gives an idea of how cramped the blocks were. A public domain image by Peter Tóth from Pixabay.

Chapter 12

Baretski approaches Lale the next morning and has the bizarre suggestion of putting on a football match, as Lale narrowly avoids being caught with his contraband goods. Baretski asks Lale to find a team of 11 to take the SS on in a friendly. Lale questions that no substitutes would be allowed, which is a bit odd, as substitutes were only gradually allowed in football matches from the Fifties and Sixties onwards. Although he is full of disgust and hatred towards the SS (especially as he has no idea of Leon's fate), Lale agrees, much to his own surprise. Baretski tells Lale that the match will be on Sunday (which means that Lale will potentially miss that week's meeting with Gita). However, as there are no transports coming in, Lale has the day off.

Lale uses his day off to sort out his contraband goods, and to purchase more food from Victor. In the evening, he goes to Block 7 to recruit some footballers for the match. Leon's disappearance does not appear to be a topic of conversation, presumably because like Pepan, people 'disappear' in Auschwitz all the time. The first response he gets is an unequivocal "no". But then a player called Joel volunteers. Lale hopes that he can get a few more volunteers by saying that this is their one chance to get physical with the SS and not be punished for it. Another prisoner called Joel says he knows someone who played for the Hungarian national team from Block 15.

The day of the match arrives, and the Joels have managed to assemble a team, six of whom have played semi-professionally. (Not a surprise perhaps, as the number of prisoners outweighs the number of SS). Joel thinks that they can win the match, but Lale tells him that they mustn't, for fear that the SS would shoot prisoners in retaliation.

Lale sees Gita, but doesn't dare go up to her. Baretski approaches Lale, and takes him to Schwarzhuber and Houstek, and introduces him as the captain of the prisoner team. An SS officer presents Schwarzhuber with a trophy that bears the legend "1930 World Cup", and suggests that they play for that. The SS officer then says that he believes that the winners were France. Obviously this SS officer is not a real football fan, as France won their first World Cup in 1998. Uruguay won the first FIFA World Cup in 1930. This is not the actual World Cup of the time, the Jules Rimet trophy, although the Nazis did try to steal it, according to Paul Gadsby in his 2014 article in *The Guardian*:

> During the Second World War the trophy was held by the 1938 winners, Italy, in a Rome bank. Fearing for its safety, the Italian Football Federation's president, Ottorino Barassi, smuggled the trophy out of the bank and into his apartment in the city. However,

51

the Nazis had followed the scent and conducted a search of Barassi's home. But they weren't thorough enough. They missed the old shoebox stashed underneath Barassi's bed, the trophy hidden inside.

(https://www.theguardian.com/football/2014/jun/13/world-cup-mystery-what-happened-jules-rimet-trophy)

So, this trophy is not the Jules Rimet trophy, but possibly a presentation trophy given to the French national team during their participation in the 1930 World Cup. Indeed, France played the first World Cup match, in which they beat Mexico 4-1, and scored the first World Cup goal. This trophy possibly came from the captain of that French team, Alexandre Villaplane, the first player of North African origin to play for France. Villaplane fell from grace after the World Cup, as he gradually became involved in the criminal underworld through betting on horse races, and was imprisoned when he got involved in fixing horse races. Villaplane gradually lost interest in his football career, so it's conceivable that he would have sold any World Cup trinkets he had to fund his gambling. Villaplane met the Nazi collaborator Henri Lafonte in prison after being arrested for handling stolen goods by the SS. This led to Villaplane being made the leader of a Brigade Nord-Africaine [BNA] in 1944, who helped the Nazis stamp out resistance groups in the south of France. The BNA was a rather paradoxical organisation, as it consisted of North Africans, who were not exactly Aryan in the eyes of any Nazi. However, the BNA were useful to the Nazi regime as it unravelled, and they were natural allies through their shared criminality. Villaplane was a vicious BNA leader, as Amit Katwala reveals in his Talksport article *World Cup 1930: the France Captain turned Nazi collaborator*:

> He would extract cash from desperate Jews and members of the resistance by offering them salvation, and then send them to the death camps anyway. "They're going to kill you – but I'll save you, risking my life," went his speech. "I've saved fifty-four. You'll be the fifty-fifth. That'll be 400,000 Francs." Those who couldn't pay were left to the BNA.

(https://talksport.com/football/124257/world-cup-1930-france-captain-turned-nazi-collaborator-14030482040/).

Villaplane was executed on 26th December 1944 by a French firing squad for the murders he had committed as a Nazi collaborator.

The prisoner team seem to have forgotten Lale's advice, and are soon winning 2-0, with the SS looking angrier and angrier. The 'master race' hasn't quite mastered football, it seems. The first half ends 2-2. Rather unsportingly, it appears that the SS team are given drinks at half time, but the prisoners are not. Lale persuades the prisoner team to ensure that they lose by one goal.

Rather gruesomely, ash from the Crematoria begins to fall on the pitch. As Heather Morris writes, "this core task of Birkenau has not been interrupted by sport". Everyone knows that people are being slaughtered in the Crematoria, but it's not commented on, as unfortunately it has become part of everyday life (and death) at Auschwitz.

Since the prisoners are so malnourished, they don't need to throw the game, as they become physically exhausted and are unable to stop the SS scoring two goals. As the game ends with a SS victory, Houstek congratulates Lale on playing well.

Although the football match might appear to be an otherwise frivolous episode, it is important to have eyewitness accounts of what life in Auschwitz could be like, such as this. Indeed, this is not the only football match that the SS played against prisoners. Walter Winter, in his 1991 book *Winter Time: A Memoir of a German Sinto who survived Auschwitz* wrote of a similar football match. An SS officer called Hartmann asked Winter to form a prisoner team. Winter is unable to find a right winger from among his Sinto and Romany compatriots, but a short Jewish man volunteers (little Joel?) who turns out to be a terrific player. Hartmann arranged for this prisoner team to have extra rations. Here is Winter's account of how the first of two matches went:

> There were six Polish national players in the Main Camp team. Kick off. Only a reduced SS presence remained in the camp, all the other SS men were at the sports field. SS lined the field on all sides as no prisoners were allowed to watch. Our camp lay directly adjacent to this sports field so we were able to watch... Everyone ran to the fence - the entire Gypsy Camp stood at the fence as spectators, with kith and kin, as the saying goes, or on the roofs of the blocks. The match began. We attacked from the start and scored the first goal after ten minutes. I thought, "Now all hell will break loose!" Normally the SS men from the Main Camp were rivals of those from Birkenau but at this moment they were sportsmen. As we scored, our SS, the Birkenau SS, began to fire off their revolvers, like fireworks going off. So now, on, on! In the

second half, we scored again. All hell did break loose! I thought, "Lad, if only you survive this!" The two SS factions began to abuse one another and were close to hitting each other. Shortly before the end we conceded a goal. We won 2-1. That eased things.

Lale meets up with Gita, and they go to their usual place behind the Administration block. Gita looks for four leafed clovers, so Lale comments that it's paradoxical for someone who doesn't believe that they are going to get out of Auschwitz to look for good luck charms. Gita reveals that there is a practical reason for this search, as the SS are very superstitious, and giving a four leafed clover to a SS could be enough to prevent a beating. They flirtatiously play with the grass. Lale asks if he can kiss Gita. Although neither of them has brushed their teeth in a very long time, they do embrace in a kiss, which is only interrupted by the sound of a dog barking. They rapidly disentangle, as the dog would have a handler.

As they go back, they see Cilka in the woman's camp, who's looking very pale. *Spoiler Alert!* Some readers will know that there is a sequel to *The Tattooist of Auschwitz* called *Cilka's Journey*. From reading the back cover blurb, it's clear that Cilka survives Auschwitz, although obviously she has to endure great suffering. Lale is puzzled as to why Cilka is looking so pale, but obviously readers will know of the sexual violence that she has been subjected to by Schwarzhuber.

Although Lale is disturbed by Cilka's appearance, he is thrilled by Gita calling him "My Love".

Chapter 13

Lale and Gita go to their separate beds, enthralled by their developing passion for each other. Cilka lies numb while Schwarzhuber molests her. Commandant Rudolf Höss sips a Grand Vin, while a drunken Baretski shoots out the light in his room. (It's true that discipline at Auschwitz was so lax that Baretski was not the only SS man who would lazily resort to shooting out his light at the end of the night. This is a detail that Heather Morris looks to have sourced from the 2005 BBC series *Auschwitz, the Nazis and the Final Solution*, which was handily being shown on the Yesterday channel as I was writing this book.)

When he goes to the Administration block the next morning, Lale sees that Cilka is still very withdrawn, and he resolves to ask Gita what is wrong with her.

Lale is met outside by a hungover Baretski, who tells Lale that they have to get a truck to Auschwitz. Once there, Baretski abandons Lale to have a lie down, and tells him to go to Block 10. Having looked up Auschwitz Block 10, I see this is where SS doctors conducted experiments on prisoners. My immediate thoughts are that Lale has been sent to collect Leon (dead or alive), or that Mengele has an errand for him. Lale is sent to the back of the block by an SS officer, and is shocked to see dozens of spaced out girls lying around. Since Heather Morris uses the word "girls", these appear to be children, instead of young women.

Heather Morris writes: "Lale watches as a guard comes into the enclosure and walks through the girls, picking up their left arms, looking for a number, one possibly made by Lale." Now, readers will remember that when Lale and Leon were ordered to process the Romany families, they were relieved when no child gave them an identification number to transcribe on their arms, although Lale observed that some of them appeared quite young. Now, there is documentary evidence that children were tattooed at Auschwitz, so I wasn't sure if Lale had ducked away from admitting that he had tattooed children. Lale held back from telling his story for so long for fear of being accused of being a collaborator. It seemed to me that he may have been holding back in his account of tattooing the Romany families by not admitting to tattooing children, for fear of being accused of abusing children. However, as I wrote in that earlier section, it's likely that Lale and Leon would have been summarily executed if they had refused to tattoo children. Many Auschwitz prisoners had to do unsavoury acts to survive, such as Cilka. As I've written earlier, the SS intentionally demoralised the prisoners further by making them do their dirty work; i.e.by forcing prisoners to harm each other.

Lale is ordered to go inside by another SS officer, and finds more semi-conscious prisoners lying around. Lale announces himself to a "nurse", who looks at him disgustedly. He follows her into a room, where Mengele is examining a multitude of young girls. Since Mengele is described as grasping breasts in his examination of these young girls, it would appear that they are young women after all, or at least post pubescent.

Mengele orders Lale to tattoo the girls that he is "keeping". One suspects that those young girls dismissed to the Crematoria would endure less suffering. Mengele threatens Lale: "One day soon, Tatowierer, I will take you." Possibly Mengele just says this for his own cruel enjoyment. Perhaps Mengele only says this in his own domain, where Lale has less "protection" from the Political Department (not that this helped Leon).

Mengele tells the frightened young girls not to worry; this is a hospital, they will be looked after. Obviously, Lale has seen evidence to the contrary; not that he can say anything about this. This is most likely Mengele's sick humour.

Once Lale has finished tattooing, he sees that the enclosure out back is emptied, the young girls within presumably disposed of.

Gita goes back to her block that night to find that there are some new arrivals. Heather Morris tells us that the prisoners resent the new arrivals, who they are sure have been better fed than them, as they have only just arrived. Gita is surprised to see an older woman coming towards her (as most older women are exterminated in the Crematoria upon arrival at Auschwitz).

The woman is Hilda Goldstein, one of Gita's neighbours from her hometown of Vranov nad Topl'ou. Hilda tells Gita that her parents and sisters were taken several months ago. Gita's brothers had joined the resistance prior to this. Gita collapses as she realises that her parents and sisters are dead. However, Gita resolves to only sacrifice a few tears for her parents and sisters, determined not to let their murderers take any more than that from her. Gita embraces Hilda, which acts as a bridge for the prisoners to accept the other newcomers.

Hilda tells Gita that the people back home knew of the concentration camps, but had no idea of the industrial scale of the slaughter – just that people weren't coming back. Despite that, only a few had sought refuge in a neighbouring country. (They probably realized that there were no safe havens in neighbouring countries, such was the reach of the Nazis at the time.)

Gita realizes that Hilda won't last long in Auschwitz, so she promises her kapo a diamond ring from Lale if Hilda is allowed to stay in the block all day, as long as she empties the toilet buckets at night.

Lale goes to Auschwitz every day for the next few weeks, as there are many prisoners to process, despite the five Crematoria working to full capacity. This means that Lale has no chance to see Gita in the Administration block, and has no way of letting her know that he is safe.

Baretski is happy for a change, and tells Lale that the prisoners are all going to be given extra rations and blankets for a few days, as the Red Cross are coming to inspect the camp. Lale wonders to himself if the outside world would finally learn of what was happening at Auschwitz.

Lale asks Baretski if he can pass on a message to Gita to let her know that he is okay, and Baretski promises to do this. Although Lale and some other prisoners do get some extra rations, Lale is unsure if the Red Cross ever visited the camp.

This could be a reference to an anticipated visit to Auschwitz by the Red Cross to the Czech family camp at Birkenau, also know at the Theresienstadt family camp. Starting from September 1943, transports of Czech Jews from Theresienstadt concentration camp began to arrive at Auschwitz. These new arrivals were given special treatment:

> On arriving at the camp they did not undergo the usual selections, and families were also not divided up into various sections in the camp - hence the "family" camp. The "privileges" also included the fact that the [Theresienstadt] prisoners were not subjected to the humiliating ritual of having their heads shaved on arrival, and that children were allowed to spend daytimes in a children's block.

(https://www.holocaust.cz/en/history/events/the-terezin-family-camp-in-auschwitz-birkenau/)

Now that the outside world was becoming aware of the presence of concentration camps, such as Auschwitz, the Nazis came up with a ploy to quell the rumours about mass exterminations. They asked the Czech family camp prisoners to write back to their families and friends in Theresienstadt to say that they were okay ahead of a visit by the Red Cross to the

Theresienstadt ghetto in 1944. The Nazis spruced up the Theresienstadt ghetto prior to the visit of the Red Cross to give their visitors the false impression that it was a thriving cultural community. An anticipated follow-up visit to Birkenau didn't happen. Once it became clear that the Red Cross were not going to visit Birkenau, the SS sent the inhabitants of the Czech family camp to the gas chambers. According to holocaust.cz, "The liquidation of the family camp on 8 March and 10-12 July 1944 was the largest mass murder of Czechoslovak citizens during the Second World War."

Lale finally gets a chance to race over to the Administration block, and finds that Baretski didn't deliver his message to Gita, so Gita thought he was dead. Lale tells Gita that he loves her. Gita points out that her once lovely hair now looks horrible, but Lale says that he will love how it looks in the future. Gita protests that they have no future (i.e. will not survive).

Dana and Ivana are pleased to see Gita looking so happy again, and advise her that she should let Lale know that she has lost her family. Gita says that she prefers not to tell Lale, as the time she shares with him are the only moments when she can escape from thinking about Auschwitz. Gita agrees not to keep any secrets from Dana and Ivana.

Block 10. Public domain image by alanbatt from Pixabay.

Chapter 14

The next morning, Lale collects his supplies from the Administration block, but tells Bella not to give him too much, so that he can come back more often. Lale notices that Cilka's chair is empty.

Another missing person turns up when Lale goes to the selection area, as Baretski has brought a rather broken Leon along with him. Lale is tremendously relieved and embraces Leon. He promises to fatten Leon up. Leon confirms that it was Mengele that made him suffer, and that he wasn't merely depriving him of food. Leon reveals that Mengele had him castrated.

There were experiments in sterilization being run at Auschwitz at this time. For instance, the Nazi doctor Horst Schumann experimented in using x-rays to sterilize men and women prisoners. With two x-ray machines pointed at their sexual organs, most of the victims suffered severe radiation burns, and were then gassed in the Crematoria. The Nazis started out sterilizing people with genetic illnesses from 1933 onwards. Germany wasn't the only nation state doing this at the time, with the United States leading the way from 1890 to 1920. And it mustn't be forgotten that when he was found guilty of public indecency (of being homosexual) in 1952, British war hero Alan Turing was given the option of chemical castration to avoid being sent to prison. Having chosen the former, he committed suicide two years later.

The Nazis believed that the Germans with the 'best' genes had been killed during World War I, which had allowed people with weaker genes (i.e. those who didn't fight) to reproduce, weakening the German genetic gene pool as a result. It's inevitable that the Nazis would have experimented with industrialized sterilization as part of their bid to wipe out Jews in the 'Final Solution'. Mengele mostly carried out operations without anaesthetic, so the operation to castrate Leon must have been unbearably painful for it, along with the psychological damage of not being able to reproduce. This is another facet of Lale's shock in the face of this revelation; as Lale dallies with the idea of consummating his passion for Gita, he must suddenly have a nightmare vision of even this little fantasy being taken away from him. It's estimated that by 1945, up to 450,000 people may have been sterilized by the Nazis. (https://www.thoughtco.com/sterilization-in-nazi-germany-1779677).

Leon asks for his old job back, and Lale gladly agrees, on the condition that Leon builds up his strength before resuming duties. Lale sends Leon to his room to take whatever food he wants.

There are no transports the next day, so Lale has the day off. He persuades

59

the kapo from Block 7 to let Leon stay there, on the understanding that Leon would work for him when he regained his strength. (Although Leon had previously lived there, when he took Lale's place in the block, so I'm not sure why Lale has to negotiate to get Leon back in there).

Baretski finds Lale and tells him that he has work to do. Lale says that he'll have to go back and get his tools, but Baretski says he won't need them. Lale is very worried when it becomes apparent that Baretski is leading him in the direction of the Crematoria.

Baretski tells Lale that there are two prisoners with the same number, so Lale has to help sort out who is who. Baretski sardonically calls Leon "the Eunuch".

They enter the Crematorium, and Lale sees some Sonderkommandos, the prisoners that the SS have tasked with disposing the bodies from the mass exterminations. Lale has conflicting thoughts about encountering them. "He tries to make eye contact with them, to let them know he too works for the enemy. He too has chosen to stay alive for as long as he can, by performing an act of defilement on people of his own faith… Their lives parallel his and he feels a sinking in his gut at the thought that he too is despised for the role he plays at the camp. Unable to express in any way his solidarity with these men, he walks on."

The Sonderkommandos, like others who worked for the enemy, were given very little choice about the matter, as they would be executed if they refused. According to Gideon Greif's 2005 book, *We Wept Without Tears: Interviews with Jewish Survivors of the Auschwitz Sonderkommando*, often the first job of the Sonderkommando was to dispose of the bodies of his predecessors, as the SS kept Sonderkommandos alive for 3 months before consigning them to the gas chambers. Only those with special skills were allowed to live longer. The Sonderkommandos were given better rations, living conditions, and freedom from summary execution only because the SS depended on them to be fit enough to keep the Crematoria running.

Baretski leads Lale to one of the gas chambers and reassures him that all the gas is gone. Lale and Baretski say "After you" to each other, as Lale doesn't really want to go into the midst of the chamber's horrors. Heather Morris writes: "Bodies, hundreds of naked bodies, fill the room. They are piled up on each other, their limbs distorted. Dead eyes stare. Men, young and old; children at the bottom. Blood, vomit, urine and faeces. The smell of death pervades the entire space."

Baretski is unusually mute and so another officer does the talking, asking how two prisoners can have the same number. Taking a closer look, Lale points out that one of the numbers have faded, so each prisoner has a different identity number after all.

Lale is physically heaving after the horror of such a sight. "You *bastards*. How many more of us must you kill?" Lale asks Baretski, angry that the young SS man apparently feels nothing. Baretski confirms Lale's feelings by stupidly joking that Lale is probably the only Jew who has walked into a gas chamber and come out alive. Even more stupid when one considers that the Jewish Sonderkommandos go into the gas chambers all the time in order to dispose of the bodies.

A recreation of an Auschwitz Crematorium. Public domain image by alanbatt from Pixabay.

Chapter 15

Now that Lale has seen the worst of humanity, he feels emboldened to seize the day. He uses his work for the Political Department to go past the SS to Block 29. Lale then bribes Block 29's kapo to bring Gita to him. Baretski has apparently ordered the kapo not to interfere with Lale and Gita's romance.

However, when Gita arrives, she is furious with Lale. Having been escorted there by SS, Gita and Cilka thought that she was being taken away to be killed. She runs over to beat him to express her anger. However, the anger eventually subsides, and turns into passionate lovemaking, as they finally consummate the bond between them.

Gita wants to talk about why Lale looked so upset when she first came in, but Lale doesn't want to break the mood by revealing the horror that he saw in the gas chambers. Gita suggests that they could meet up again the next day, but Lale says that they had better not. (To do any more would be very risky.)

As Lale leaves, the kapo thanks Lale for the chocolate, and asks for sausage.

While it may seem improbable that Jewish prisoners would be able to have sex at Auschwitz, this is not the only instance of this happening, as Helena Citronova relates in Laurence Rees' *Auschwitz: The Nazis and the 'Final Solution'* (2005):

> "The Jewish [male] prisoners fell in love with all kinds of women as they worked. They disappeared once in a while into the barracks where the clothes were folded and they had sex there. They would have a guard so that if an SS came they could be warned."

I'm not quite what these Jewish men would be doing in the Canada warehouses, unless it they were delivering the goods stolen from the new arrivals. Indeed, there is photographic evidence that the stolen goods were delivered to the Canada warehouses by male prisoners.

Readers may recall that I was puzzled by the mention of young boys gathering up the personal possessions of the new arrivals when Lale first arrived at Auschwitz. There were young men, teenagers probably, that kapos used as their dogsbodies and for more sinister purposes, as Herman Langbein wrote in *People in Auschwitz* (2004):

> A remedy for sexual distress that was customary in other concentration camps, in which no women were interned next to

men, was frequently used in Auschwitz as well. Kapos kept Pipel, young fellows who in return for their personal services were exempted from hard labour and enjoyed other privileges. Quite a number of kapos abused their boys sexually.

And as Laurence Rees writes in *Auschwitz: The Nazis and the 'Final Solution'* (2005): "The young boy was a 'pipel' – camp slang for the young servant of a kapo (and someone with whom the kapo often had a homosexual relationship")". Although the Nazis despised homosexuals, they would tolerate the sexual abuse of children in this way. For it was the SS way to make life more intolerable at Auschwitz by encouraging the prisoners to abuse one another.

So, it's just as well that Gita's kapo is acting as a guard for Lale and Gita as they make love, for one would presume that the SS would not tolerate consensual sexual relations between adult Jewish prisoners.

A row of Birkenau blocks. A public domain image by Peter Tóth from Pixabay.

63

Chapter 16: March 1944

We've leapt ahead in time somewhat, missing out a whole winter. Lale is woken up by two young Polish men knocking on his door. They tell him that one of their friends escaped last week, but got caught, and they're worried about how he's going to be punished. They think the Tatowierer might be able to help.

Lale tells them that their friend was stupid to get caught, and thinks that he'll be hanged, as this is the punishment for trying to escape. Lale doubts that he can do anything to help, as all he has access to is food. Lale asks them where the escapee is, and it turns out that he's just outside the block. Presumably he's not under guard, as he's already "under guard" by being back in the camp. Lale asks him to tell how he escaped. The young man says he was working outside when he needed to defecate, and one of the guards told him to do it in the forest. When he saw his work detail walking away, he feared being shot if he ran to join them, so just went back into the forest. He got caught when he walked into a village to steal some food, since it was very obvious where he had come from due to his tattoo.

Lale thinks for a moment and then goes to the Administration block to ask Bella about a transport that is going out that night. Bella confirms that there is a transport going to a "boys' camp", where no one is tattooed. By "boys' camp", it's clear that Bella means a camp for men, as she wonders if Lale wants to be on it at first. (Like the chapter when Lale tattoos Mengele's experimental subjects, Heather Morris's uses of the words "girls" and "boys" makes you think that she's writing about children, when she is in fact writing about men and women; or, at the very least, adolescents.) Since this transport will consist of new arrivals that haven't been tattooed, their names are used on the "passenger" list instead of identity numbers. Lale has to go back to his room to find out the name of the young man (Mendel Bauer). Although one would have thought that he could have been better to use a fake name, as surely Mendel's name is already in the Administration block's records, linked with his prisoner identification number? A number that is still tattooed on him. However, Lale has thought of this, as he changes the tattooed number into a picture of a snake. Lale does question if a guard would double check a name that has been handwritten at the bottom of the transport list, but Bella says that the guards wouldn't want to get into any bother. (Although it is not long since Lale's trip into the gas chamber to check out a similar administrative anomaly.) Lale gives Bella a ring encrusted with gemstones in compensation for taking such a risk.

Lale goes back to his room, and tells the young Polish men his plan.

Although the conditions in the new camp are certain to be grim, at least it won't be the certain death that Mendel faces at Auschwitz. Lale sees to it that Mendel gets on the transport safely. Obviously, the SS would have discovered that Mendel had escaped again, and it's possible that (as was their way) they would have retaliated for this by killing some other prisoners from Mendel's block.

While it's nice to know that Lale may well have helped a prisoner escape certain death, there are a few gaps in this story that make it seem a little incredible. But who knows? While corruption was rampant amongst the SS at Auschwitz, stupidity was probably rife too. So it's possible that an SS man wouldn't bother to check a handwritten name on a list from the Administration block in the early hours of the morning.

This is some of the electric fencing at Birkenau. Public domain image by Marie Sjödin from Pixabay.

Chapter 17

Heather Morris starts this chapter by saying that many prisoners die due to malnutrition, disease, or by exposure to the cold. (Although it must be gradually getting warmer, as the previous chapter was set in March. Then again, the prisoners are so malnourished that it wouldn't take much to kill them.) It's true that the electric fence at Birkenau contained enough voltage to kill you, and that some prisoners escaped from their suffering by running into the fences to commit suicide. (They were either electrocuted on the fence, or shot by the tower guards as they ran towards the fence.) Heather Morris states that tens of thousands of prisoners are being sent to Auschwitz.

Lale and Gita are still managing to see each other on Sundays, and sometimes are able to find some quiet time alone together in Gita's block. When Lale and Gita had their first passionate tryst, they didn't use protection, so one does wonder if they did use some form of contraception. Auschwitz was certainly no place to bring up a baby. Even more so when you consider that many children born in Auschwitz were murdered shortly after birth, according to Polish midwife Stanislawa Leszczyńska. She spent two years in Auschwitz after she and her family were caught helping Jews in her home city of Lodz. She volunteered her services as a midwife when she arrived in the camp. Leszczyńska's skills as a midwife saved the lives of many women in the squalid conditions. She was ordered to kill the newly born children, but refused. However, there were others did agree to do this, according to www.history.com:

> "Sister Klara," a midwife who had been sent to the camp for murdering a child, oversaw the barracks with a woman named "Sister Pfani." They were in charge of declaring babies born in the ward stillborn, then drowning them in buckets, often in front of the mothers who had just given birth.

(https://www.history.com/news/auschwitz-midwife-stanislawa-leszczynska-saint)

This was another way that the SS used prisoners to demoralise fellow inmates. If the babies looked "Aryan", then they could be taken away and given to Nazi parents. It is believed that the Nazis stole about 100,000 children from Poland as part of this Lebensborn programme. Leszczyńska and other nurses tattooed such children, in the hopes that they could one day be reunited with their parents (so it looks like Lale would not have been tattooing new-borns). The above website states that pregnant woman were often summarily executed, so Lale and Gita are running a huge risk. One might consider that Gita was so malnourished that it is unlikely that she would conceive; but malnourished women do give birth. Besides, Gita has more access to food than most at Auschwitz through Lale's black marketing, and Heather Morris comments that Gita's kapo has been getting fat from the food that Lale's been giving her as payment for allowing these visits.

Gita finally tells Lale that Schwarzhuber is sexually abusing Cilka. Gita says that both she and Cilka keep a track of their monthly cycle to ensure that they're not having sex when they're most fertile. (One can only presume that Schwarzhuber doesn't want a child, and so doesn't molest Cilka when she is at risk of pregnancy. One supposes that it would be problematic for a senior SS officer to have a Jewish baby, as they were not supposed to have sexual relations with Jewish women.) Indeed, this 'relationship' is one of the main criticisms of the novel by Wanda Witek-Malicka from the Auschwitz Memorial Research Centre in her article *Fact-checking The Tattooist of Auschwitz* in *Memoria* 14, November 2018: "The disclosure of such a relationship would have involved an accusation of race dishonour (Rassenchande) and severe punishment for the SS man." She quotes Gerhard Palitzsch as an example, but Palitzsch was punished for theft as much as sleeping with a non-Aryan. Josef Garlinski relates in *Fighting Auschwitz* (1975) that Palitzsch only began sleeping with a Jewish prisoner after his wife had died of typhoid fever, although one does wonder how consensual this relationship was.

Readers with long memories will recall that Amon Göth, commandant of the Płaszów concentration camp, was depicted in Thomas Keneally's 1982 novel *Schlinder's Ark* (and in the *Schlinder's List* film directed by Steven Spielberg), as having sexual desire (i.e. raping) his Jewish maid, Helen Hirsch:

> Schindler raised his voice now… "He won't kill you, because he enjoys you too much, my dear Helen. He enjoys you so much he won't even let you wear the Star. He doesn't want anyone to know it's a Jew he's enjoying. He shot the woman from the steps because she meant nothing to him…. But *you*…. It's not decent, Helen. But it's life."

Keneally suggests that one of Göth's SS subordinates knew about him sexually abusing Helen Hirsch, but it was not sexual relations with a Jew that got Göth into trouble with the SS hierarchy, but his smuggling of contraband goods and his harsh treatment of his SS subordinates. Göth had two maids called Helen. The other one, Helena Sternlicht, denied that Göth was sexually attracted to them, and just beat them brutally. However, Helen Hirsch was one of the sources for *Schlinder's Ark*, so it looks like Keneally got this directly from her.

Franz Wunsch and Helena Citronova nearly got caught out, as Citronova related:

> But inevitably, since over time "all Auschwitz" knew about their feelings for each other, someone informed on them… She was taken to the punishment bunker in Block 11. "Every day they took me out and threatened me that if I didn't tell them what had gone on with this SS soldier, then at that very moment they would kill me. I stood there and insisted that nothing had been going on." Wunsch had been arrested at the same time and, like Helena, under questioning denied that any relationship existed. So eventually, after five days of interrogation, both of them were released.

(*Auschwitz: The Nazis and the 'Final Solution'* by Laurence Rees, 2005)

As Wanda Witek-Malicka points out, Heather Morris does not provide any biographical details about the real life Cilka, Cecília Kováčová. We can't be sure that Cilka is actually Jewish, and we probably won't find out until *Cilka's Journey* is published. Readers will recall that Gita met Cilka in the Administration block, and then took her back to meet her friends in Block 29, so she wasn't part of the Jewish transport that Gita arrived on. If Cilka was Jewish, then it's possible that Schwarzhuber was so senior that he thought that he could get away with having sexual relations with a Jewish woman, especially because he was abusing her, instead of having a romantic relationship with her. Hermann Langbein writes:

> Hoffman, who had been a friend of his colleague Schwarzhuber since their service in Dachau, told me that Schwarzhuber was the only person who told Höss straight to his face that he had not joined the SS to kill Jews. When I asked Hoffman whether Schwarzhuber was drunk when he said that, he denied it.

(*People in Auschwitz* by Hermann Langbein, 2004)

Langbein also reports this judgement of Schwarzhuber by Czeslaw Mordowicz: "It was possible to imagine worse people than him. Personally, Schwarzhuber was not as brutal as the others." Before we get too carried away with this image of Schwarzhuber as a reasonable human being, Langbein records that Schwarzhuber only had this image as a "caring commandant" as he ordered SS men and prisoners to carry out acts of

68

brutality, to avoid getting his own hands dirty. Obviously, the one act of brutality he didn't order his subordinates to carry out was his sexual abuse of Cilka.

We do know that Schwarzhuber had a family at Auschwitz, as Baretski revealed at the Frankfurt trial:

> When he was asked whether children of SS men were permitted inside the camp, he answered in his clipped, harsh speaking voice:…"There was Schwarzhuber's boy, he was six years old, and when he went to the camp to look for his father, he had a sign around his neck that said he was the son of SS camp leader Schwarzhuber so they wouldn't grab him and send him to the gas chamber…"

(*People in Auschwitz* by Hermann Langbein, 2004.)

It's unlikely that Schwarzhuber was abusing Cilka every night, as he had a wife and family at the camp. Commandant Rudolf Höss also had a 'mistress' at the camp, an Austrian political prisoner called Eleanor Hodys:

> In Auschwitz, he began to pay special attention to an Austrian prisoner, Eleanor Hodys, a non-Jewish seamstress who had been caught forging a Nazi document. When she was working in his villa, he startled her by kissing her on the lips, causing her to lock herself in the bathroom. Soon she was locked up in a cell in the interrogation block. Careful to avoid detection by his own guards, Höss started visiting her in secret; she resisted him again at first, but then gave in. She became pregnant, and was moved to a dark, tiny cell in the basement, where she was kept naked and given minimal food. When she was finally released, she was six months pregnant and, at the commandant's behest, sent to a doctor who performed an abortion.

(*The Nazi Hunters* by Andrew Nagorski, 2016)

Thomas Keneally writes about this incident in *Schlinder's Ark* (1982), when writing about the SS hierarchy's investigation of Amon Göth's corruption: "They had even attempted to find evidence for the arrest of the renowned Rudolf Höss, and had questioned a Viennese Jewess who, they suspected, was pregnant by this star of the camp system." At the beginning of this book, I wrote how *Schlinder's Ark* had been considered too factual to be considered a novel. Yet, if Keneally was referring to Eleonore Hodys in the above extract, then he made a mistake by writing that she was Jewish. As previously written, it's not possible to write such long narratives as this without making mistakes, and the Booker Prize winning *Schlinder's Ark* looks to contain factual errors too. This is why I'm not so harsh on mistakes by Heather Morris; although her publishers could have tidied up many of them without derailing Lale's narrative.

Going back to Lale and Gita's sexual relationship, a woman trying to avoid "accidents" by keeping a record of her monthly cycle is not exactly fool proof. By 1944, there was a gynaecologist in Auschwitz that could perform abortions, called Gisella Perl. Obviously, having a "back street" abortion was dangerous in the 1940's, even more so in the squalid conditions of Birkenau. Perl thought that she had no option to do so, as she was forced to work for Mengele:

> "The greatest crime in Auschwitz was to be pregnant," Perl once said. In the name of "science," Mengele took special glee in experimenting on expectant mothers, conducting sadistic tests that eventually killed both the woman and her child. Initially unaware of Mengele's agenda, Perl was ordered to report every pregnancy to the doctor himself. Mothers were also tricked into trusting the Angel of Death with promises of better nutrition… But when Perl discovered the doctor's true intentions, she "decided that never again would there be a pregnant woman in Auschwitz."

(https://knowledgenuts.com/2014/07/28/the-auschwitz-abortion-doctor-who-saved-thousands/)

Gisella estimated that she performed 3,000 abortions in order to save the mothers' lives. The babies would have been doomed anyway, so Gisella did what she could to save the mothers. Most of these mothers appeared to have conceived their children prior to their arrival at Auschwitz – I couldn't find any references to children that were conceived by prisoners at Auschwitz, apart from Eleanor Hodys. Investigating these abortions online is complicated by the fact that several anti-abortionists have now taken to calling abortion a "holocaust". While they are entitled to express their views strongly, I don't think it's helpful to use the extreme circumstances of the holocaust as a metaphor.

Lale calls Cilka a "hero", but Gita is annoyed by this, saying the Cilka just wants to live. Lale says that choosing to live is an act of defiance against their Nazi abusers.

Lale then addresses his working for the Nazis: "I have been given the choice of participating in the destruction of our people, and I have chosen to do so in order to survive. I can only hope I am not one day judged as a perpetrator or a collaborator." Such sentiments explain why Lale kept his silence for so long, for fear of being accused of being a collaborator.

The kapo tells Lale off for being in the block when the other women return, due to the risk of their "little secret" being exposed.

Lale is called over by Victor and Yuri, who have some provisions for him. So much indeed, that they can't fit them all in Lale's bag, so Lale stuffs food into his clothes. Heather Morris then relates that there is another woman in Birkenau who has been allowed to keep her blonde hair. Commandant Höss was very taken by her at one of the selections, and ordered that her hair should not be shaved. Lale sees this blonde woman as he heads back to his block, with a sausage shoved down his trousers... I'm not sure if Heather Morris intends this as a double entendre or not? Similarly, I thought there was a possibility of this when Gita's kapo asked for some "sausage" after Lale and Gita first consummated their passion. However, these events are related in such a matter of fact way that it's hard to tell if any humour is intended.

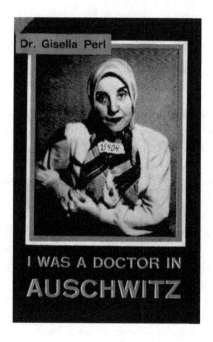

71

Chapter 18

Heather Morris reveals that it's spring, and the warmer weather gives the camp's inhabitants some renewed hope. Even Baretski has a spring in his step. He quietly asks Lale for a favour, saying that he knows that Lale can get things from outside. Baretski says that he hasn't shot Lale because he likes him, and because they're like brothers (which must really make Lale squirm with disgust). Baretski reveals that he's taken Lale's advice, and has been writing nice things to his girlfriend. Baretski asks Lale if he could get some nylon stockings for his girlfriend; American company DuPont first mass produced nylon stockings in 1939, so this synthetic fabric was still very new. Nylon was also used to manufacture tents and parachutes during World War II, and American servicemen would give nylon stockings to their overseas girlfriends. So, they would have been quite tough for Lale to get hold of. For a girlfriend who has previously loved wearing Baretski's uniform, nylon stockings would have been redolent of the enemy; but they were the must-have fashion item for a woman of the time.

(https://www.thoughtco.com/history-of-nylon-stockings-1992195)

Lale cringes when he hears Baretski using Gita's name. However, there is no work for Lale today. Lale goes looking for Victor, but Yuri tells him that his father is a bit ill at the moment. Fortunately, Yuri is confident that he can get his hands on some nylons. It probably helps that Lale gives him a couple of diamonds.

Lale is walking over to the women's compound when he and others see a US Air Force plane circling above the camp. The watchtower guards are nervous due to all this commotion. Some of the prisoners point at the Crematoria and futilely ask the plane to drop bombs on the gas chambers.

Lale ducks out of the way before the watchtower guards begin shooting the crowd. Lale decides to lay low instead of visiting Gita.

Lale goes back to his block and finds that some of the Romany children have been shot during the commotion. Lale is asked to bring the other children inside, so that they don't have to see their dead playfellows before the SS have the bodies disposed of. However, the children are in trauma and are aware that something terrible has happened. One of the men asks Lale what the SS are going to do with them, to kill them? Lale says, "Not if I can help it." The fate of the Romany camp is well known, though, as previously written. Lale gives the children some chocolate, but they are too shocked to celebrate this rare treat.

Lale goes outside to help the men put the children's bodies into piles for the SS to have taken away. Some mothers refuse to give up the bodies of their dead children, but they are wrenched away anyway.

"Yisgadel veyiskadash shmei rabbah" – is indeed part of the Mourner's Kaddish in Jewish culture.

Lale reveals that it is the 4th of April 1944. That is indeed that date that the Allies first took aerial photographs of Auschwitz. However, the pictures were taken by the South African Air Force, not the US Air Force:

> On 4 April 1944, a Mosquito plane from 60 Photo Recon Squadron of the South African Air Force flew out of Foggia base in Southern Italy to photograph the factory. It was the IG Farben factory at Monowitz, only 4km from Birkenau. In order to ensure complete coverage of the target, it was common practice to start the camera rolling ahead of time, and stop it slightly over time. As a result, the Auschwitz camp was photographed for the first time. During that same period, the Allies had commenced planning a comprehensive attack on the German fuel industry, and the Monowitz factory was high up on the list of targets.

(https://www.yadvashem.org/yv/en/exhibitions/through-the-lens/auschwitz-aerial-photos.asp)

This does appear to be a factual error in *The Tattooist of Auschwitz*. However, the South African Air Force did carry out the aerial photography on the behalf of the US Air Force.

The IG Farben factory at Monowitz plays a huge role in the Auschwitz story, as the camp would never have grown to such a size without the factory. The factory was founded at Monowitz due to the great supply of natural resources that were vital for IG Farben's wartime enterprise:

> The history of the founding of the camp is connected with the initiative by the German chemical concern IG Farbenindustrie A.G. to build its third large plant for synthetic rubber and liquid fuels... Among the several sites proposed in December 1940/January 1941, the final choice fell on the flat land between the eastern part of Oświęcim and the villages of Dwory and Monowice. The decision was justified by the favourable geological conditions, access to railroad lines, water supply (the Vistula), and the availability of raw

materials: coal (the mines in Libiąż, Jawiszowice, and Jaworzno), lime (Krzeszowice), and salt (Wieliczka). Furthermore, the belief that it would be possible for the firm to employ prisoners from the nearby Auschwitz concentration camp…. may in fact have been decisive in the choice of the project.

(http://auschwitz.org/en/history/auschwitz-iii/ig-farben)

Lale realises that it will soon be two years since he arrived in Auschwitz. He wonders how it is that he has survived while so many others have perished. Lale believes this is down to his resolution from the start to survive, and to make the SS pay for their crimes. He thinks that the sight of the plane today is a sign of the endgame, with the possibility of eventual rescue. Lale remembers the night sky as a boy, and the lovely nights when he entertained ladies as a young man. Lale thinks that his family will be looking at the night sky, and hopes that they get more comfort from the stars than he does now. It doesn't seem to occur to Lale that his family are most likely dead.

Lale reflects back on the last time he saw his family in March 1942. He relates that he had left his job and apartment in Bratislava the previous October. He had done this after being warned by a friend in the government that Jews were soon going to be treated more punitively in the Slovak Republic. Lale reveals that he was offered and took the job as assistant to the leader of the Slovakian National Party, as he was advised that this was the best way to escape persecution. Lale wore the uniform of the Slovakian National Party, which was much like a military uniform. Unfortunately, there were very many young men who took up wearing Nationalist uniforms in the first half of the Twentieth Century, something which very much contributed to the two World Wars.

Lale relates that the main purpose of the party was to keep the country in the hands of Slovakians. It helps that the Slovakian National Party was denouncing the government of the time for not standing up to Hitler and for not offering "protection to all Slovaks" (i.e. Slovakian Jews). There are very few websites that detail the history of the Slovakian National Party, but most of them agree that it was effectively swallowed up (along with most other political parties in the Slovak Republic) by the Slovak People's Party in 1938. The Slovakian National Party didn't really exist in February 1942, so the outfit that Lale joined must have been quite a fringe group at this time. Had Lale not been in Auschwitz, it's likely that he would have been one of the Slovakian youth that turned against Tiso's government. Indeed, there was internal resistance to Tiso's regime from the start:

74

The shortage of qualified personnel enabled resistance members to infiltrate all levels of the Tiso administration, where they promoted economic sabotage. Mutiny within the Slovak army (marshalled by the Axis powers for combat against Poland and, later, the Soviet Union) was encouraged and became commonplace. At Kremnica, on September 15, 1939, approximately 3,500 Slovak soldiers abandoned their transport train and marched into the city. Members of the underground Slovak Revolutionary Youth set fire to machinery in factories, emptied the fuel tanks of locomotives, and exploded munitions in warehouses. Slovak youth turned increasingly against the Tiso regime.

(*Czechoslovakia: A Country Study* by Ihor Gawdiak, Federal Research Division, 1989)

Jews in Slovakia had been ordered to wear the yellow Star of David when out in public, but Lale had refused to do this, as he saw himself as a Slovakian first, with his religion being an incidental part of his make-up. Again, Heather Morris reiterates the image of Lale being a ladies' man, when she states that his Jewishness "was a matter discussed more often in the bedroom than in a restaurant or club".

Lale relates that he was given advance warning that the German foreign ministry had requested the transportation of Jews out of the Slovak Republic as a labour force in February 1942. Lale asked for leave to visit his family and was told that he could return to his job in the party at any time.

Lale discloses that the prevailing view of Jews in the Slovak Republic was that they thought that the Nazis wouldn't invade as the government was already giving them everything they wanted. Although they were aware of the Nazis committing atrocities against Jews in other small countries, Slovakian Jews didn't believe that they were particularly at threat, despite the restrictions placed on them by their own government.

Lale struggles to comprehend how two communities – the Romany and Jews – that have spread over a variety of countries, could ever be seen as a threat as they did not have the military potency of a nation state.

75

Chapter 19

Gita asks Lale if he has lost his faith. Gita thinks that he has and this saddens her. Lale says he lost his faith due to all the horrors that he witnessed when he first arrived in Auschwitz. (Although Lale appeared numb to all the suffering at the time, this reveals that it did have an impact on him.) Lale says that the only thing he believes in both of them getting out together. Lale refuses to be defined as a Jew above everything else. Gita says that Lale would have a say in her keeping her faith. Indeed, Lale very much encourages her to keep hold of her faith, so that she can pass it to her babies. To which Gita replies that she doubts that she'll have babies as she thinks she's "screwed up inside". Lale says that once they've escaped, he'll fatten her up, and they will have beautiful babies. Gita thanks him for giving her hope for the future. Lale then asks her again for her surname, but she declines once more, and says that she'll tell him on the day they leave. One suspects that something will get in the way of this revelation that will lead to them having problems meeting up again.

Lale then goes to spend some time with Leon and his friends from Block 7 on what is a beautiful summer's day. When he goes back to his room, Lale realises that something is wrong when the Romany children do not greet him. He finds two SS officers inside, who have discovered his contraband jewels. Knowing how corrupt the SS are, one hopes that they will just steal it. But no, they dump the jewels into his bag and lead him away at gunpoint. Lale thinks that he is leaving the Romany camp for the last time – and perhaps he is – just not for the reason he thinks.

Lale is brought before Houstek, who asks him who gave him all this jewellery. Lale says other prisoners gave them to him, but he doesn't know their names. Infuriated, Houstek says that he'll have to get someone else to do the job of Tatowierer now, and orders his men to take Lale to the notorious Block 11 at the main Auschwitz camp. Block 11 was the block where Auschwitz inmates were tortured and punished for wrongdoing. It's also where the SS first experimented with using Zyklon B. Although one small glimmer of hope for Lale is that he's not being sent immediately to the gas chambers. Even so, Lale feels this is the end, and mentally begins to say goodbye to his loved ones. He pictures his father with his beloved horses, to whom he always spoke so warmly "in contrast to the way he expressed himself to his children". This is the first hint we have that Lale's relationship with his father is not as close as that with his mother. Perhaps Lale is Oedipal in this regard after all, by having a dislike for the same sex parent.

Lale is placed in a small cell in Block 11. This is not one of the worst cells in

Block 11, as there were cells in which prisoners only had room to stand up in. Prisoners were placed in these standing cells overnight (in which they obviously couldn't sleep), and then were forced to go to work the next day. Such a punishment could be repeated for night after night.

Heather Morris then writes that "The reputation of Blocks 10 and 11 are well known. They are the punishment blocks." However, this appears to be an error, as we've already seen Block 10 in the novel, as this is where Mengele (from 1943) and other SS doctors carried out their cruel, unethical medical experiments. The prisoners in Block 10 suffered a great deal, but they were not being punished: they just had made the mistake of being twins, fertile, pregnant or non-Aryan. Lale probably didn't know this, but the Black Wall (or "Death Wall") had not been used for executions for some time, on the instructions of Commandant Arthur Liebehenschel, who had run Auschwitz from December 1943 to May 1944. Indeed, since Heather Morris has told us that it a lovely day when Lale was arrested, it's likely that the Black Wall had already been demolished on the orders of Liebehenschel, a detail that Lale probably didn't pick up on when he was shoved into Block 11. Liebehenschel also discontinued the use of the standing cells in Block 11, and prisoners were no longer sent to the gas chambers on his watch. It's quite possible that Lale is lucky to be punished during the "lighter hand" of Liebehenschel's time in command. Obviously thousands of new arrivals were still sent to the gas chambers while Liebehenschel ran Auschwitz, which is why he was executed for crimes against humanity in 1948. Heather Morris later relates that Lale was punished for smuggling from 16th June to 10th July 1944, when Rudolf Höss was back in charge of Auschwitz.

During his third day in the cell, a large man comes in and gives him broth. Lale is relieved to recognise the American strongman Jakub, whom he fed on his first day in Auschwitz. Lale hasn't seen him since he was taken away on the orders of Houstek while showing off his muscles. Lale finds that he can't stomach the weak potato broth that Jakub has given him. Lale jokes about Jakub needing more food than most. Lale speculates that someone who missed out from his food distribution informed the SS about his smuggling activities. Unfortunately, it turns out that Jakub's job is to torture prisoners who have information that the SS require, and that this is what Jakub does to survive. Lale is suddenly not so keen on the man he once helped. This is the kind of prisoner-on-prisoner violence that the SS deployed to demoralise the prisoners further. It was much easier to get a prisoner to their dirty work for them, than to suffer any guilt or remorse from carrying out such beatings themselves.

Jakub says that he will kill Lale before he can reveal the names of his fellow smugglers, to reduce the amount of innocent blood on his hands. Such are the awful ethical quandaries that prisoners had to take, such as Gisella Perl, who aborted babies at Auschwitz so that the mothers would live, instead of both baby and child being murdered by the SS.

Lale is despondent that this is the awful work that the SS forced Jakub to do. Jakub tells Lale to speak Yiddish, as the SS here don't know that he speaks German. Lale is resigned to his fate, to be beaten to death at Jakub's hands. Lale wonders if Gita will ever find out what has happened to him.

Lale's dreams take him back to his childhood home. Lale's father is angry that Lale failed to turn up to work, meaning that Lale's father had to do all the work by himself. Lale runs behind his mother, who protects him from his father's ire. His mother says that she'll punish Lale after supper, to which Lale's brother and sister roll their eyes, as they've heard this all before. Lale promises to help his father more, but finds this difficult, as he doesn't want to end up like his father, "too tired to pay his wife a simple compliment about her looks or the food she spends all day preparing for him." Perhaps if Lale had helped him, his father would not have been too tired to do this?

As a child, Lale used to sometimes say that he would marry his mother when he grew up. (Again this mother/son love theme.) As he grows up, Lale asks his mother what he should do to be a good husband (unlike his father). She tells Lale to always listen to his wife, no matter how tired he is. He should learn what his wife likes, and give her little treats. Lale asks how he will know which woman will be the right one for him, and his mother reassures him that he will know.

When Lale wakes, he acknowledges forlornly that Gita is the one for him.

Later on, Jakub drags Lale to a windowless cell, which contains handcuffs and a birch rod. There are two SS officers in the room, who don't pay Lale much attention until Jakub starts beating him. Quite a few of the blows that Jakub lays are exaggerated, to look worse than they are. Jakub tells Lale to pretend to faint, which is not too difficult when Jakub punches Lale in the stomach. The disinterested SS officers are satisfied with what they've seen, and seem to believe that Lale doesn't know the names of the other prisoners that have been smuggling with him. So Jakub doesn't have to beat Lale to death after all.

Jakub takes care of Lale for the next few days while he recovers from his injuries. Lale reveals that the beating was severe enough for him to be marked for life, and thinks perhaps that this is due punishment for having worked for the Nazis as the Tatowierer. Lale asks Jakub if he broke his nose, but Jakub says he still looks handsome enough for the girls, to which Lale replies that he has already found "the one".

The next day, two SS officers come for Lale. He is relieved at first when it becomes apparent that he is not for the Black Wall (which may not still be standing). Lale can hardly stand upright after a week in the cells, as he is led to a truck that takes him and other prisoners back to Birkenau. Lale doesn't think for a moment that he's being transported to the gas chambers, presumably because selections for inmates at Auschwitz had been stopped by Liebehenschel.

This is a recreation of the Death Wall between Blocks 10 and 11. A public domain image by Jacek Abramowicz from Pixabay.

Chapter 20

Lale is brought back before Houstek. The two SS officers carrying Lale reveal that not even torture from Jakub was sufficient to get the names of his fellow smugglers out of him. Houstek is a bit surprised that the SS didn't just shoot him. So Lale is now his problem again. Houstek tells the SS officers to take Lale to Block 31.

Now, Block 31 is where youth worker Fredy Hirsh set up the Children's Barracks as part of the Theresienstadt family camp. As readers will recall, Theresienstadt was the Czech Jewish ghetto that the Nazis had gentrified in preparation for a visit by the Red Cross. Jewish families were transported from Theresienstadt to Auschwitz and were given privileges, such as keeping their own clothes and not being shaved. This was all part of an anticipated visit by the Red Cross to Birkenau, in which the SS intended to deceive the outside world of the horrifying true nature of their concentration camps. While the first arrivals from Theresienstadt in September 1943 were sent to the gas chambers in March 1944, there were still many surviving from the December 1943 transport in early summer 1944, although they anticipated being gassed six months after their arrival, just as their predecessors had been. Most of the December 1943 arrivals from Theresienstadt were gassed during 10-12 July 1944, when it became clear that the Red Cross were not intending to visit Birkenau (so the SS had no need to maintain the façade of decency that the family camp had been intended to portray).

Sometime prior to Fredy Hirsh's death in March 1944, the children's barracks put on a show of *Snow White* in German, which several SS officers attended. Hirsh's ability to interact with SS officers may well have saved the lives of some of the children, who would have found it harder to kill children that they had got to know.

(https://www.haaretz.com/world-news/europe/.premium.MAGAZINE-the-unknown-hero-who-saved-children-at-auschwitz-1.5976721)

During the Frankfurt Auschwitz trial, Baretski gave evidence to this account:

> In his ponderous speaking style, this defendant gasped out the following: "There was the Theresienstadt family camp, and it was common knowledge that this camp was to be gassed. There were children too: they established a children's theatre, and we had already gotten used to these children. When the camp was supposed to be gassed we (evidently, several block leaders) went to see the SS camp leader and said, "But not the children, too?" It was a

group of sixty-eight or seventy children. SS camp leader Schwarzhuber saved the boys by putting them in the men's camp."

(*People in Auschwitz* by Hermann Langbein, 2004).

Baretski also claimed that he had pleaded for the lives of the girls to be saved, but Dr Lucas (who had jurisdiction over the women's camp) refused.

Even if Block 31 was no longer being used as the Theresienstadt children's barracks in early summer 1944, it would still have been part of the Theresienstadt family camp. Either that, or Lale is sent there after 12th July 1944, when presumably the SS had filled up Block 31 with other prisoners. I had anticipated that Lale would have been caught in the slaughter of the Romany camp, but it's possible that he might be involved in the massacre of the Theresienstadt family camp. However, it's clear that Houstek means to punish Lale by forcing him to undertake hard labour when he's nearly been beaten to death. So Lale being sent to Block 31 at this time looks to be an error in the novel for the reasons above.

The two SS officers toss Lale into Block 31 after Lale collapses on the way. Lale doesn't seem to care that the skin from the top of his feet are scraped off by this, so worn out is he by his beating and lack of food from the previous week.

One of the prisoners recognises that Lale is the Tatowierer, and says that he was always handing out food around Block 6, where this prisoner previously came from. So, Lale's friendliness to other prisoners and handing out of food may well save his life here, as two of the prisoners share their food with him. One of the prisoners states that he irritated someone when he first arrived, so that he's only known Block 31. So, this does seem to reinforce the idea that Heather Morris made a mistake by setting these scenes in Block 31, as the novel gives the impression that these prisoners have been in the block for a while. It appears that prisoners are sent to Block 31 as punishment, for the labour they are expected to do must be even harsher than the usual Birkenau work.

Lale tells the two prisoners that he needs to get out of the block, but they tell him that the only way out is to throw himself on the death cart, or be shot for collapsing while working next day.

That night, Lale dreams of his departures from home. He first left to get a fulfilling job in Bratislava, to travel Europe, and to find the woman of his dreams. His second departure was the one that brought him to Auschwitz. He tells how he went to Prague as instructed in mid-March 1942. On 16th April 1942, he was ordered to go to a local school where young Jewish men from all over Slovakia were being housed. Lale made sure that he washed his clothes every day, so keen was he to remain well-dressed.

After five days, the men were ordered to go to the railway station. Lale relates that some of his fellow Jews refused to go into to the cattle trucks at first, but that those who resisted had rifles pointed at them by the Slovakian army guards, soldiers from their own country. (I'm still not sure why the transport was from Prague, as Prague wasn't part of the Slovak Republic, but the Protectorate of Bohemia and Moravia at the time. Surely the soldiers would have been Czech instead of Slovaks? Then again, these soldiers would have been his countrymen before Czechoslovakia was broken up, and would be his countrymen again when Czechoslovakia was restored as a nation state after World War II.)

The two prisoners from Block 31 help Lale during the morning rollcall. It's been a long time since Lale had to do rollcall, and obviously he's still worn out from his beating at the hands of Jakub. Since Lale is the newest occupant of Block 31, his number is called last.

Lale then finds out what his new 'job' is: to carry rocks from one side of a field to the other. The SS shoot the prisoner who is lagging behind each time (a rather unpleasant 'game').

Lale manages to survive the day, although on one occasion he was the penultimate prisoner. Lale is excused the task of carrying back the dead bodies for one day only.

Lale sees Baretski waiting for him as he arrives back at the Birkenau gates. Baretski says that he had heard what happened to Lale as way of explanation for his presence. Lale is not comfortable consorting with the enemy in the presence of his fellow prisoners, but necessity dictates that he must ask a favour of Baretski – to tell Gita where he is. Baretski is uncomfortable doing this, and thinks it's probably better Gita thinks Lale dead is already, instead of being in the "notorious" Block 31. However, Lale insists, and directs Baretski that he must ensure that Gita knows to tell Cilka; presumably because Cilka is in the position to ask favours from her abuser, Birkenau Commandant Schwarzhuber. It's just as well that Gita finally told Lale what was upsetting Cilka, as this little detail could be the one thing that keeps Lale alive.

Baretski jokes about the treasure trove of contraband that Lale had gathered before his arrest. (South Africa used pounds as a result of being a British territory.)

This time, Baretski does pass the message on to Gita, who passes it in turn to Cilka. Gita is greatly relieved to hear that Lale is alive.

Sure enough, when Cilka is in bed with Schwarzhuber that night, she runs the risk of asking him just one favour, as she has always done everything that he has wanted, and has never asked him anything before.

Lale manages to survive the torturous game the next day, and thinks himself selfish for only thinking about the pain of carrying one of the dead men. As he arrives back, he sees Cilka standing next to Schwarzhuber on the other side of the fence. Schwarzhuber points out Lale to one of his guards, who then asks Lale to follow him. All the other inmates of Block 31 stare at Lale as he is led away. The guard tells Lale that he's been commanded to take him back to his old room in the Romany block. (So, it looks like Lale will be there to see the demise of the Romany family camp. I guess it would have been a bit confusing if Block 31 had turned out to be the Theresienstadt family camp in the novel, as having Lale witness the demise of the two family camps would have been a bit too much.)

Lale makes his own way back, and is greeted by those who thought he was dead. Lale makes contact with Nadya, before retreating to his room, for fear of being overcome with the emotions that accompany his reprieve.

Chapter 21

Lale wakes up to find Baretski leaning over him, who jokes about him being a cat with nine lives. Baretski says it must be nice having friends in such high places, although Lale counters that he'd "gladly give my life for her not to need such friends", since Schwarzhuber is Cilka's abuser, not her "friend".

Baretski jokes that Lale thinks he runs the place, and says that he's never known anyone else walk away from the Strafkompanie. The Strafkompanie ("punitive unit") was the system of very hard labour that the Nazis employed in concentration camps. Here, Baretski could be referring to the Strafkompanie of Block 11, Block 31, or both. Heather Morris later reveals in the "Additional Information" section at the end that Lale was in the Strafkompanie from 16th June to 10th July 1944.

Baretski says that Lale has his old room back as it goes with the job of Tatowierer. Baretski is very dismissive of Leon being Tatowierer in Lale's absence. He advises Lale not to go near Houstek, as he had wanted Lale to be shot.

Lale suggests getting hold of some chocolate as a way of thanking Cilka, but Baretski warns him that he'll be watched like a hawk from now on, so it wouldn't be wise to do any more smuggling. (Heather Morris later states that the Political Department began to pay Lale for his work as Tatowierer sometime after his release from the Strafkompanie. The Nazis did reward some 'valued' prisoners in concentration camps, and one of the incentives for non-Jewish male prisoners at Auschwitz was a visit to the camp brothel, with sexual services provided by female prisoners. Heather Morris says that Lale didn't know what to do with this money, so he gave it to Baretski to buy chocolate from the officers shop to give to Gita, Dana et al. Obviously Lale did not appreciate being paid by the Nazis for a job that he had little option but to do, since this would make him look even more like a collaborator.)

Lale apologises for having been side-tracked from getting Baretski's nylons, but the SS man says not to worry as he's been dumped. Baretski reassures Lale that the break-up wasn't due to any of his romantic advice, as his ex-girlfriend had hitched up with someone else in her own town. (Evidently this was a long distance relationship all along, and not a fling that Baretski had with one of the SS women at Auschwitz.)

Leon is delighted to have Lale back again.

The next afternoon, Lale takes the chance to see Gita as the women leave the

Administration block. Gita and Dana warmly embrace him. Lale gives thanks to Gita and Cilka for having saved him. Lale promises to never leave Gita again. Lale walks Gita back to her block, as they dare not be late, as Lale no longer has anything to bribe her kapo with. Lale asks Gita to hang on in with him, as they will have a life together after Auschwitz. Gita has doubts that they can plan any life together, as neither of them knows what tomorrow will bring. Lale can't bring himself to tell her the details of his recent suffering. Lale insists that they will leave this place and get married.

As he goes back to his block, Lale is approached by two young prisoners from Block 9 who ask that he get them some more food, and give him a diamond.

The next morning, Lale takes the risk of meeting up with Victor and Yuri again. Lale gives Victor the diamond, and explains that he won't be doing quite as much business with them as previously. Lale asks Yuri if he has any chocolate, and the young man hands some over to him.

Lale then heads over to the women's camp. Lale jokes with Gita's kapo about not having seen her for a while, and how she's lost some weight. The kapo asks a female SS officer to fetch Gita. Although Lale doesn't want to talk about his beating, he takes off his clothes to show Gita his scars. Then they make love, and Lale reveals that this is the deepest love he's ever known.

Chapter 22

Lale relates that he's been spending hot summer days with Gita. Lale's workload is heavy, as thousands of Hungarian Jews have been sent to Auschwitz. Hungary was an ally of Nazi Germany, and had benefited from rising German power to recover some land that the Austro-Hungarian Empire had lost after World War I, including areas of Czechoslovakia. Later on in March 1939, Hitler allowed Hungary to occupy Carpatho-Ukraine. Under Nazi pressure, Hungary had started enacting anti-Jewish laws from 1938 onwards. By 1944, the government of Hungarian Regent Miklós Horthy had begun approaching the Allied powers with a view to surrendering unconditionally, as the Red Army was already on Hungary's borders. In March 1944, the German Army invaded Hungary. Horthy was advised that he could only stay as Regent if he appointed a pro-Nazi government. It was this new government that began the deportation of hundreds of thousands of Hungarian Jews to Auschwitz from 14th May 1944 to 24th July 1944. Hungary had previously been a safe haven for Jews fleeing from Nazi persecution in neighbouring countries, but this changed with the invasion of the German army, with devastating effect:

> Almost one half of all the Jews that were killed at Auschwitz were Hungarian Jews who were gassed within a period of 10 weeks in 1944.

(https://www.scrapbookpages.com/AuschwitzScrapbook/History/Articles/Hu ngarianJews.html)

Lale says that these new arrivals have caused unrest in the camps, with the established prisoners resentful of the influx of newcomers. "The higher the number on a person's arm [i.e. the latest arrivals], the less respect they receive from everyone else." In the women's camp, the Hungarian Jews are resentful of the perks that the long-term Slovakian Jews have managed to negotiate. Heather Morris reveals that the Slovakian Jews have been allowed to keep casual clothing from their Canada warehouses, and so are no longer wearing the striped pyjamas. Although, when there are disputes, the SS punish the long-term Slovakian inmates as much as the new Hungarian arrivals.

Gita and Dana keep out of the fights. Gita has to be especially careful, as her "safe" job in the Administration block, her friendship with the influential Cilka, and the private time with boyfriend Lale are all potential causes of jealousy.

Lale is mostly separated from these camp tensions by working for the Political Department, and by living in the Romany family camp. Lale relates that he gets on well with the young Romany fathers, and the older Romany women, who seem to look after everyone. However, he doesn't have good friends with the older Romany men, who he finds remote, just like his own father.

And so the fateful night of August 2nd 1944 arrives. Lale wakes up to the sound of the Romany family camp being rounded up by the SS. It's a bit odd that Lale doesn't say anything about the previous time the SS tried to liquidate the Romany family camp (maybe he was working overtime with the arrival of the Hungarian Jews):

> When, in May 1944, SS guards attempted to liquidate "gypsy family camps" in Auschwitz, they met with unexpected resistance—the Roma fought back with crude weapons—and retreated. A few months later, however, the SS returned and succeeded in gassing the remaining prisoners. Twenty thousand Roma were killed in Auschwitz.

(https://www.momentmag.com/roma-in-the-holocaust/)

Lale sees Nadya, and pleads with her not to go, but she has no choice in the matter, and she's herded away before she can say her last words to him. Lale asks an officer where they are taking them, but only gets the suggestion that the Tatowierer could be taken there too if he wanted. Lale can get no sleep that night, despite (or because of) the unusual deathly silence in the block.

Commandant Rudolf Höss wrote this regarding the liquidation of the Romany family camp:

> It was not easy to get them into the chambers. I did not see it myself, but Schwarzhuber told me that no extermination of the Jews had been so difficult, and he had a particular hard time of it because he knew almost all those inmates well and had a good relationship with them.

(*People in Auschwitz* by Hermann Langbein, 2004)

This kind of incident shows why the SS had previously stopped selections for inmates, as it was so much harder for them to kill people they knew instead of the new arrivals off the cattle trucks that they hadn't got to know as people yet.

87

Lale has to perform his duties the next day. Mengele decides to especially torment Lale and Leon. Obviously, he has already castrated Leon, so Lale's understudy would always have reason to fear Mengele's approach. As Mengele was the lead doctor for the Romany family camp until its liquidation, he would know exactly why Lale would be so upset today, and so takes it upon himself to provoke Lale even further by threatening to take him away.

Lale feels ash from one of the Crematoria fall on him and he loses control. Mengele notices and starts to walk back towards the tattooists. Lale can only think of Nadya. Of course, Lale hasn't personally known anyone who's been sent to the Crematoria before, so it's no wonder that he has problems keeping his emotions in check, especially as there were men, women and children that he knew in the Romany camp who had been gassed. Lale drops his tattooing stick, and in the commotion, Mengele comes to confront Lale. Mengele holds his pistol to Lale's forehead, forcing Lale to address him directly. Mengele has possibly never shot anyone in cold blood before, but such is his reputation for clinically disposing of prisoners in monstrous experiments, that Lale is wise not to put this to the test. Fortunately, Lale is able to placate Mengele.

When he goes back to his block, he finds that its new inhabitants are some of the Hungarian Jews that he tattooed earlier in the day. Lale doesn't make any attempt to build links with them, for what would be the point of that? Despair is never far away in Auschwitz.

Chapter 23

Gita struggles to console Lale over the loss of his Romany family over the two months, such is Lale's despair. (Readers who know their Auschwitz history will realize the exact time period from an event that happens later on in this part of the narrative.) Gita tries to cheer him up by getting him to talk about his previous life back home, but Lale refuses to do so unless she divulges more about her own past. (Again, I can't help think that this may hamper their reunion after the camp.) Gita has never seen Lale so low.

She points out that it's more than just the Romany family camp that have been wiped out, and they have the evidence that thousands more have been killed. Lale realises that the people that he tattooed were just numbers to him, while Gita sees them as people with names and identities. From her job in the Administration block, Gita knows a lot more about the collateral history of prisoners that have passed through Auschwitz than he does.

Lale promises not to be so gloomy, as obviously the slaughter has always been going on around them. Gita tells him that he would honour his dead Romany family by surviving.

However, a big explosion shakes the ground beneath them. It's Saturday October 7th 1944, and the Sonderkommando, having learnt that they are due to be killed as part of their 4 monthly rotations, are rebelling. There was a resistance movement within the camp, which had been planning to blow up the Crematoria for some time:

> For months, young Jewish women, like Ester Wajcblum, Ella Gärtner, and Regina Safirsztain, had been smuggling small amounts of gunpowder from the Weichsel-Union-Metallwerke, a munitions factory within the Auschwitz complex, to men and women in the camp's resistance movement, like Róza Robota, a young Jewish woman who worked in the clothing detail at Birkenau. Under constant guard, the women in the factory took small amounts of the gunpowder, wrapped it in bits of cloth or paper, hid it on their bodies, and then passed it along the smuggling chain. Once she received the gunpowder, Róza Robota then passed it to her co-conspirators in the Sonderkommando, the special squad of prisoners forced to work in the camp's crematoria.

(https://www.ushmm.org/learn/timeline-of-events/1942-1945/auschwitz-revolt)

The Sonderkommando had guns that had smuggled into them by local partisans, which is how they were able to put up a small scale gunfight with the SS. Crematorium Four was indeed blown up using the gunpowder that had been smuggled in. The plan was for a general revolt to coincide with the approaching Red Army's arrival; however, many in the Sonderkommando thought that they would not live to see that day, so they set their plans into motion earlier than originally planned.

(https://www.jewishvirtuallibrary.org/the-revolt-at-auschwitz-birkenau)

The SS are obviously fearful of a general revolt, and they start shooting indiscriminately at prisoners leaving the Administration block, so Lale and Gita have to take cover. Lale persuades Gita that she'll be safer going back to her block, as there will obviously be a rollcall. Lale promises to find Gita the next day. Heather Morris told *The Guardian* newspaper that she had used dramatic licence in this scene:

> "Ninety-five per cent of it is as it happened; researched and confirmed... What has been fictionalised is where I've put Lale and Gita into events where really they weren't. They weren't together when the American planes flew over the camps... I put him and Gita together for dramatic licence."

(https://www.theguardian.com/books/2018/dec/07/the-tattooist-of-auschwitz-attacked-as-inauthentic-by-camp-memorial-centre)

Although Heather Morris references the scene where the aerial photography plane flew over Auschwitz, I think she was actually referring to the Sonderkommando rebellion, as Lale and Gita weren't together in the novel when the plane flew over. (Lale decided against going to see Gita once the watchtower guards opened fire.) Readers will have to remember that Heather Morris wrote the book (and the story as a screenplay) quite some time ago, so I think it's understandable that she doesn't always remember all the details exactly from a "past" book, especially while she would have been engrossed in the final details of *Cilka's Journey* when she made the above comment. Having written several books myself, I know that I can't exactly recall everything that I have written in previous works, so I can't be judgemental on Heather Morris for this.

When he goes back to his block, Lale discusses what had happened with its new Hungarian inhabitants. They tell him that some women prisoners working in the munitions factory had managed to get small amounts of gunpowder out by tucking it into their fingernails. Wanda Witek-Malicka from the Auschwitz Memorial Research Centre in her article *Fact-checking The Tattooist of Auschwitz* in *Memoria* 14 criticises this claim that the ammunition factory workers smuggled out gunpowder by concealing it under their fingernails, but this is an aspect of the story that has been doing the rounds long before Heather Morris came across it, so she can't be accused of being a source of this rumour. For example, here is the same detail published in *The New York Times* in 2014:

> Three Polish Jews assigned to work in a munitions factory just outside the Auschwitz death camp — Estera Wajcblum, Regina Szafirsztajn and Ala Gertner — were recruited by Roza Robota, who worked at the camp's clothing depot, to smuggle gunpowder to members of the Sonderkommando... The powder, carried under the women's fingernails, in their pockets and even on corpses... Three SS guards were killed; the women, after months of torture (during which they refused to give up any names), were hanged in front of inmates in January 1945, three weeks before Soviet troops arrived.

(https://www.nytimes.com/2014/11/16/arts/dance/jonah-bokaers-october-7-1944-at-center-for-jewish-history.html)

It's a pity though that Heather Morris just focused on the fingernails aspect, instead of the other methods of smuggling that were a lot more believable. It's true that the Sonderkommando had made makeshift grenades by using sardine tins (remember that they had better rations than the rest of the prisoners). The Hungarian prisoners say that they knew about the plan for a general uprising, but that they thought it wasn't due to happen that day. They reveal to Lale that the Red Army is advancing on the camp, and that the revolt was planned to coincide with their arrival. Obviously Heather Morris is using dramatic licence here, as it's unlikely that the Hungarian Jews would know anything about this tightly knit plot by the Auschwitz resistance, and that they would then spill the beans to someone who works with the Political Department. The SS retaliated by shooting many of the Sonderkommando who had not rebelled. The above details of the plot were discovered by the SS in their own investigations, so anyone with knowledge of the rebellion would have been keen to keep the details to themselves, to avoid other conspirators being punished.

Lale curses himself for not having made friends with the Hungarians earlier, as he could have used their foreknowledge of the revolt to keep Gita out of danger that day. (Although, since these Hungarians didn't know it was going to happen that day, it wouldn't have actually made much difference). Lale

91

questions the Hungarians as to when the Red Army are going to arrive, and is given some optimism from their responses, especially as these new arrivals know more about what has been happening in the outside world than he does. Lale resolves to ask Gita to keep a look out in the Administration block for any data that would suggest that liberation is indeed coming.

The rail tracks leading to the infamous Birkenau "Gate of Death". Public domain image by **Ron Porter** from Pixabay.

Chapter 24

Heather Morris relates that the autumn is very cold. Lale and Gita are optimistic now that they know the Red Army is near, and Gita shares this news with the women in her block. However, as it gets colder, the women in the block find it hard to be positive as they face another year in Auschwitz. There are fewer transports, so prisoners such as the Sonderkommando fear that they will be executed earlier than expected. Local builders such as Victor and Yuri are no longer needed in the camp, as construction work is halted. So Lale has less contact with the outside world. Heather Morris writes that "Lale has heard promising news that two of the Crematoria damaged in the explosions by the resistance fighters are not going to be repaired". Wanda Witek-Malicka in her article *Fact-checking The Tattooist of Auschwitz* in *Memoria* 14 criticises this revelation, as only one Crematorium was destroyed in the Sonderkommando rebellion. However, while this is an historical fact, I must point out that it's perfectly legitimate for Heather Morris to report a rumour going around the camp that two Crematoria had been destroyed. One mustn't let fact checking get in the way of what Lale believed to be true at the time. Although we know now from the historical record that only Crematoria IV was put out of action by the Sonderkommando revolt, it's still interesting for the historical record that the Auschwitz inmates thought that the rebellion had been more successful than it actually was.

By this time, it's the SS who are dismantling the Crematoria themselves, to stop the outside world from finding out about their mass executions, as Laurence Rees relates in *Auschwitz: The Nazis and the 'Final Solution'* (2005):

> When the end came, it came quickly, one night in January 1945, as ten-year-old Eva Moses Kor and her twin sister Miriam lay in their bunks at Auschwitz-Birkenau, they were suddenly awoken by a huge explosion... The Nazis had blown up the crematoria. Moments later they were forced out of their barracks and marched with the other twins, all of whom had been subject to Dr Mengele's experiments, down the road to the Auschwitz main camp... Above them they saw distant flashes of artillery, and in the darkness the SS harried them on without respite.

Lale reveals that more prisoners are being shipped out of Auschwitz (supposedly to other concentration camps) than arriving.

"Shipped out" is not the phrase I'd use, as most of the remaining prisoners

93

were forced to evacuate Auschwitz via the use of "death marches" to Gliwice (which was 30 miles away), or to Loslau (35 miles away) in temperatures of minus 20C. These occurred from January 17th to the 21st. Any of the prisoners who lagged behind were shot. It's thought that as many as 15,000 of the 60,000 prisoners who went on the death marches died. The Nazis took the prisoners on these death marches as they still desperately needed slave labour to carry on their war effort. Despite this need for workers, the SS still shot so many prisoners due to their own frantic attempt to escape the Red Army.

(https://www.ushmm.org/learn/timeline-of-events/1942-1945/death-march-from-auschwitz)

So Heather Morris has very much got her timelines wrong when she writes that Lale meets up with Baretski on "a late January day" to ask where Leon has gone. Baretski suggests that Lale might find himself on a "transport" out of Auschwitz. (Although the prisoners were being marched out on foot, for many prisoners the purpose of these marches was for the SS to get them to a rail junction where they could be loaded onto whatever rail trucks were there.) The Red Army liberated Auschwitz on 27th January, so this meeting can't be that late in January. Just a small edit to say that this was "early" January would have made this passage more historically accurate.

Lale thinks that he can possibly avoid being transported out, as he doesn't have a daily rollcall, but he worries that Gita will be sent away. Thinking that Leon is mostly likely dead, Lale challenges Baretski by using an odd mirror metaphor that doesn't really work. Lale foresees a time when Baretski's world will be pulled apart (since the Red Army is practically at the Auschwitz gates at this moment in time, this isn't exactly prescient). Baretski says that Lale could well die before then. Baretski makes an empty threat about taking Lale's life, but allows Lale to go back to the warmth. Lale vows that if ever he met Baretski on equal terms, then he would have no qualms about killing the SS man. Although Baretski has helped Lale on occasions, assisting him in his romance with Gita, and has been a conduit to Lale's escape from the Penal Unit, this doesn't excuse in Lale's eyes the previous barbarity that he has witnessed Baretski dishing out on other prisoners. Indeed, when the end became clear, several of those working in the SS began to be nicer to the prisoners in a bid to save their own skins.

This is the last time Lale sees Baretski, who Heather Morris tells us committed suicide on 21st June 1988.

Public domain image of Stefan Baretski

On another morning in "late January", Gita runs up to Lale's block (that he's advised her to steer clear of due to the risks) to tell him that the SS are panicking. (Again, if this section had referred to "mid" January, then it would have been fine from an historical point of view.)

Gita wants to stay with Lale, but Lale thinks she would be safer back in her block looking for Dana. Lale says that he'll come for Gita later (although I suspect they may have trouble meeting up again). Lale says that there haven't been any new arrivals for weeks, so he thinks that this could be the beginning of the end.

Lale goes to the Administration block, and sees that it's chaos in there, as the SS take all the camp records away from the inmate workers. One of the office staff tells Lale that the camp is going to be emptied, starting from the next day, as the Russians have nearly reached Auschwitz.

Lale goes to Block 29 as promised and tells Gita, Cilka et al that the SS are destroying records and that the Russians are nearby. He doesn't tell them that the camp will be evacuated, as he doesn't know where they will be evacuated to.

Lale says that he hopes that the SS run away, leaving the prisoners in Auschwitz. He tells the women not to leave the block, in case the SS guards are trigger happy, and he says that he will try to bring back more news.

Lale thanks Dana for being Gita's friend, for keeping Gita going when things have been rough. In case any reader wonders what happened to Ivana, she is there too.

Lale turns to Cilka and says to her that she's the bravest person that he's ever met. He tells her not to be guilty, and that's she an "innocent". (Having read the blurb for *Cilka's Journey*, Heather Morris's follow up to *The Tattooist of Auschwitz*, it's evident that Cilka will be accused of collaborating with the Nazis, and she will suffer for this.) Cilka says that she did what she had to survive, and it was rather that she should suffer at the hands of Schwarzhuber than some other unfortunate. Lale thanks Cilka for saving his life.

It's pretty evident to Gita that Lale is saying all his goodbyes now, in case he doesn't get to see them the next day.

Lale looks at his female friends and sees that all of them have been damaged by their experiences here. None of them are yet 21-years-old. Again Heather

Morris uses the word "girls" when she really means teenagers or young women. Their lives have been totally derailed from the ones that they should have lived. Heather Morris states in the "Additional Information" section that Gita was only 17-years-old when she arrived in Auschwitz. According to an article in *The Guardian* (1st February 2019) about *Cilka's Journey*, Cilka was only 16-years-old when she arrived in 1942, so these women have suffered awfully in what should have been their formative years.

Lale searches for Baretski, but can't find him, so he goes back to his block to tell the Hungarian inmates all that he knows.

That night, the SS come into the women's camp and paint a red slash on the back of the women's coats. Gita, Dana, Cilka, and Ivana take comfort that they all have the same markings on their coats, so they will share the same fate.

Lale is awoken by gunfire in the night, which takes him back to when the Romany families were taken away. Lale goes outside and sees that thousands of women prisoners are being lined up in rows. One woman is knocked over by a dog, and its SS handler just shoots her. Lale searches everywhere for Gita, and finally sees Gita and all her friends, except for Cilka. (I thought at first that Schwarzhuber may have arranged for Cilka to have a separate route out of Auschwitz. However, Schwarzhuber was transferred to Dachau in November 1944, and then to Ravensbruck in December 1944. He surrendered to the US army on 29th April 1945. Schwarzhuber was hanged by famed British executioner Albert Pierrepoint on 3rd May 1947 after having been found guilty of gassing women prisoners while at Ravensbruck. (http://www.redcap70.net/A%20History%20of%20the%20SS%20Organisati on%201924-1945.html/S/SCHWARZH%dcBER,%20Johann.html)).

Lale sees that Gita is finally crying, but she's too far away for him to comfort her. Dana points Lale out to Gita. So fixated is he on Gita that Lale doesn't notice an SS officer swinging his rifle butt at his face. Gita and Dana try to make their way to Lale, but they can't make their way through the huge volume of women heading in the opposite direction. Despite his head blow, Lale carries on into the crowd, and gets within an arm's length of Gita before another SS soldier puts the muzzle of his gun into Lale's chest. As all seems lost, Gita finally shouts out that her full name is "Gita Furman", and Lale is thankfully able to pick this out from all the chaos and the din. Lale shouts out to Gita that he loves her.

It's all suddenly over as the gates of Birkenau shut on the departing women. An SS officer unexpectedly comes over to Lale and helps him up, telling him to go back to his block for fear of freezing to death in the cold.

Lale is woken up by explosions and canon fire the next morning. Lale runs out with the Hungarians, and sees panicked SS amongst the prisoners. The main gates are wide open. Hundreds of prisoners walk through the gates without being stopped. Some of them are so weak from malnourishment that they turn back and return to their blocks. Lale walks out the gates and is caught up in a crowd heading towards a waiting train. Lale gets onto one of the wagons, and sees the SS shooting at those outside the train. Snow falls heavily as Lale catches his last glimpses of Birkenau and Auschwitz.

Chapter 25

Gita and Dana search for Cilka and Ivana as they march along with thousands of women through ankle deep snow. Although, they have to be careful, as any prisoners falling behind are shot by the SS on this death march.

The SS stop the march every so often to give the prisoners some much needed rest. Gita and Dana sit on their bottoms to give their feet a rest, despite the snow. Some of the prisoners are unable to get up again after the rest. Gradually, the numbers of prisoners are whittled away, making it harder to escape the gaze of the SS.

Dana has to stop during the night due to exhaustion. Four young women offer to help Dana, but she refuses, telling them to take Gita away with them. They drag Gita away, and Gita looks back to see an SS officer approaching Dana, who doesn't shoot, as he believes that she is dead already.

The next morning, the death march arrives next to a train. Gita surmises that cattle trucks brought her to Auschwitz, so cattle trucks will be taking her away. She finds out that the four young women that took her away from Dana are Polish, not Jewish, from different parts of Poland. There is a lone house in the distance, which the Polish girls are planning to make a run to. (For who knows where this train will be taking them to? It must have been agonising to have been so close to liberation, only for their imprisonment to continue onwards elsewhere with no end in sight.) With these kinds of thoughts running through their minds, Gita and the girls run to the house. The SS are so preoccupied with loading the cattle trucks, that they do not notice the women running away.

Thankfully the door to the house is opened as they run to it, and they are welcomed in front of the hot fire while the Polish girls explain their predicament to the homeowners. Gita stays silent, not wanting to give away that she is Jewish. The man of the house says they can't stay as the Nazis often search the house. He manages to remove the red paint from their coats, so that they are not visible as prisoners.

They hear shots outside the house, as the SS shoot all the prisoners that they do now want to take. The man gives them the address of a nearby relative and some bread and a blanket. They spend all night in the freezing woods.

It's evening before they reach the next village, and they have to ask directions from a kind woman. When they enter the house, the worried

99

homeowner tells them that they woman who gave them directions was an SS officer: "one of the cruellest people in the concentration camps." The homeowner's elderly mother gives them some soup in the kitchen. Gita can't remember the last time she was sat in such a domestic setting. As the homeowners are afraid that the SS woman will report their presence, a neighbour offers them refuge in their roof space during the night. They wouldn't be able to stay during the day, as that's when the Germans search houses, so Gita and her friends have to spend their days hiding in the woods.

The local priest asks his parishioners to bring food to the girls. After a few weeks, the Germans have retreated, and have been replaced by Russian soldiers. One day, as they are leaving for the woods, they are spotted by a Russian officer who is compassionate to their plight, and arranges for a guard to be placed outside the house, so that they no longer have to spend the day in the woods. One day, Gita is asked a direct question by one of the soldiers, and her answer reveals that she is Slovakian, not Polish. The word spreads around, and that night, a man in Russian army uniform comes to talk to Gita in Slovakian. (Presumably he's just taking an opportunity to speak in his native tongue.)

Gita and the Polish women become a bit too complacent, by staying around the fire in the evening, as one night a drunken Russian soldier comes in and tries to rape one of them. Their screams alert other Russian soldiers, who shoot the would-be rapist in the head and drag him out.

Some readers might ask why Gita and the Polish women were still so cautious after the Germans had retreated, and the Russians had taken their place. Well, the above episode gives an indication of why they had to be careful. Anthony Beevor, while writing his book *Berlin: The Downfall 1945* (2002), was shocked to discover that the accounts of the Red Army raping women as they swept through Germany had previously been understated. The Soviet soldiers seemed to use rape as a weapon against the country that had inflicted as many as 30 million casualties upon them as a consequence of Operation Barbarossa. Just as the Nazis had been merciless in their invasion of Russia, so the Soviets were just as brutal in their treatment of German women. The Nazis had previously forbidden sexual relations between German women and nationalities that they regarded as inferior, such as Russians. So the Red Army took revenge by raping German wives in front of their husbands. Beevor also believed that the obvious wealth of Germany in comparison to Russia was a factor, and another reason why the Russians despised the people that they had conquered. It's very apparent that the rape of women by the Red Army was underreported; the rape of men by enemy soldiers also occurs during such conflicts, and these are hardly (if ever reported), as men from patriarchal societies find admitting that they have been raped to be a further diminishment of their masculine ideal. Those few remaining Soviet soldiers that had been captured and brutally exploited by the Nazis at concentration camps, were not liberated, but treated as traitors by the Red Army and suffered accordingly.

Beevor points out that the Red Army didn't just rape German women, but also women from the countries that the Nazis had occupied:

> [That] Soviet troops raped not only Germans but also their victims, recently liberated from concentration camps, suggests that the sexual violence was often indiscriminate, although far fewer Russian or Polish women were raped when their areas were liberated compared to the conquered Germans... Jews, however, were not necessarily regarded by Soviet troops as fellow victims of the Nazis. The Soviet commissars had commandeered German concentration camps in order to incarcerate their own political prisoners, who included "class enemies" as well as Nazi officials, and their attitude towards the previous inmates was, to say the least, unsentimental.

(https://www.telegraph.co.uk/news/worldnews/europe/russia/1382565/Red-Army-troops-raped-even-Russian-women-as-they-freed-them-from-camps.html)

The above article states that women from this era refer to the Red Army war memorial in Berlin as the "tomb of the unknown rapist". However, we mustn't forget that other Allied forces, such as the British and Americans, also raped and sexually exploited women as they swept through Europe.

Back to *The Tattooist of Auschwitz*, this experience of sexual violence shakes the women, and they decide to move on. One of them has a sister in Krakow, so they decide to go there with the help of a very apologetic Russian officer, who lays on a truck and a driver to take them there.

They find that the sister in Krakow is still living there. However, the city is teaming with refugees who have returned from wherever the war has sent them, and nobody has any money. The women resort to stealing food from a market. One day, Gita hears a Slovakian voice in the market, and arranges a lift with this Slovakian greengrocer to Bratislava. She hopes that, while the rest of her family are dead, one of her brothers might have survived fighting the Nazis as a partisan. The other women wave her off.

Once in Bratislava, Gita lives in shared accommodation with other refugees from the camps. She registers with the Red Cross in the hope that they can put her in touch with any of her remaining family. Gita is terrified one day to see two Russian soldiers jumping in the back garden of the house she is staying at. However, she is relieved when she sees that it is her two brothers, Doddo and Latslo. They tell her that they can't stay long, as the locals are suspicious of anyone wearing a Russian army uniform. This is probably because the Soviet Union didn't support the Slovak National Uprising of 29th August 1944 against Tiso's army, probably because it was too early (the Red Army wasn't near enough), and the Soviets were distrustful of the resistance movement. The German army invaded Slovakia to defeat the uprising, and they resumed the deportation of Jews from the Slovak Republic on 30th September 1944. On 4th April 1945, the Red Army liberated Bratislava from the Germans. So, Gita's reunion with her brothers most likely happens in mid-1945.

(https://www.globalsecurity.org/military/world/europe/sk-history-4.htm)

Jozef Tiso fled to Germany as the Red Army swept through the Slovak Republic. He was put on trial by the Czechoslovak National Court, and found guilty of collaborating with the Nazis, treason, for his actions in quelling the Slovak National Uprising, and for his crimes against the Jews. He was executed on 18th April 1947:

> Zabkay witnessed Tiso's execution, which he described as botched. The gallows had no trap. Instead, a rope was tied under the obese priest's armpits and he was hoisted aloft by means of a pulley at the bottom of the post... The noose was a third rope... The rope holding Tiso's weight was dropped, the rope attached to his legs was yanked, while the hangman jerked on the noose. In theory, this technique would snap Tiso's neck. It did not. He suffocated, convulsing on the rope. A large metal crucifix reportedly slipped from his hands to the concrete floor, "resounding like a bell in the terrible silence."

(*Priest, Politician, Collaborator: Jozef Tiso and the Making of Fascist Slovakia* by James Mace Ward, 2013)

Gita decides not to tell her brothers about the fate of the rest of the family, as she doesn't want to spoil the exhilaration of this reunion. Gita jokes that she looked better in the Russian uniform that she wore when she arrived in Auschwitz than her brothers do in theirs'.

Chapter 26

Lale reveals that he has risked bringing some gems with him. He left the rest in his room back in Auschwitz. The train stops outside another concentration camp. A fellow prisoner, Joseph, tells Lale that he's been here before: this is Mauthausen in Austria. Joseph goes on to say: "Not quite as terrible as Birkenau, but nearly." Lale is probably wondering if he made a good decision to get on the train, as Mauthausen was indeed a brutal place. Here prisoners would be killed through hard labour and starvation, and all were given the label of "Rückkehr unerwünscht" ("return not desired"). The Nazis used Mauthausen as a punishment centre for prisoners that had been too troublesome in other camps, for escapees, and for anyone else that the Nazis thought were undesirable. Mauthausen also used gas vans and gas chambers.

(https://www.britannica.com/place/Mauthausen-concentration-camp-Austria)

Later Nazi hunter Simon Wiesenthal was also an inmate at Mauthausen at this time, following a death march from another concentration camp.

(https://www.biography.com/people/simon-wiesenthal-9530740)

Lale finds out very quickly how starved the prisoners have been here. Like Auschwitz, prisoner accommodation is very cramped. Having written that, there is one man per bunk, so it may not have been as overcrowded as Auschwitz. Lale and Joseph manage to find a block that isn't too full, and as this block fills up, they in turn tell newcomers to "piss off".

The next morning, Lale sees that he is to be strip searched and puts the three largest diamonds in his mouth, while scattering the rest of the gems. (Although based on events around the same time, Lale obviously hasn't read *Papillon* by Henri Charriere, as this novel was first published in 1969, in which other bodily orifices were used to hide valuables in a French penal colony. Like *The Tattooist of Auschwitz*, there has been some debate about how much of *Papillon* was true and how much of it was fiction. Charriere claimed that the events in the book were true, bar for lapses of memory. The French publisher said that *Papillon* had been presented to him as a novel, but that he persuaded Charriere that it would be better to publish it as an autobiography. Likewise, as discussed previously, Heather Morris stated that *The Tattooist of Auschwitz* is a fictionalised version of Lale's true story, after critics pointed out inaccuracies in the book.) Lale sees the guards inspecting the mouths of the prisoners in front of him, so he manages to roll the diamonds under his tongue. As his mouth is already open for inspection, the guards only momentarily glance at it.

It appears that the hard labour at Mauthausen has finished, as Lale and his fellow prisoners mostly sit around doing nothing (except starve). Lale gets to talking to an approachable SS guard, who wants to know what Auschwitz was like, and Lale gives him a sanitised version. A few days later, the guard asks Lale if he'd like to be moved to a sub-camp at Saurer Werke in Vienna. Lale is advised that the conditions are slightly better there with a laxer regime. (I couldn't find any details about Saurer Werke, so hopefully it's not one of those camps where the Nazis worked prisoners to death.) The guard tells Lale that this sub-camp is not supposed to have any Jews, so he would have to hide his religion there. Hopefully there won't be any strip searches there, as Lale would not be able to hide that he had been circumcised. (Solomon Perel, a young Jewish man, managed to masquerade as an ethnic German during the war, despite being circumcised, to the extent of joining the Hitler Youth. His incredible story of survival was released as a film in 1990, *Europa Europa*.) However, it would appear that there will be no strip searches at the new camp, as the guard just advises Lale to cover up his tattoo while at the sub-camp. Lale finally gets his name back, as it's his name on the transfer list, not an identity number. Although the guard didn't ask for anything and didn't expect anything, Lale gives him one of his diamonds. "Now you can't say you never got anything from a Jew."

On 5th May 1945, Mauthausen was liberated by the US army. It's likely that had he stayed, Lale would still have suffered – from starvation, if nothing else.

When Lale arrives at the new sub-camp, it isn't exactly the image of Vienna that he'd pictured during his days of wanderlust. (As noted earlier in the book, Vienna is very close to Bratislava, so it's a wonder that Lale didn't get a chance to visit the Austrian capital pre-war. And as Vienna is so close to the Slovak Republic, it's no surprise that Lale's thoughts turn to Gita, who, unknown to him, is not far away in Bratislava.)

The guards at the new camp don't pay much attention to Lale and the new arrivals, and just tell them where their blocks are and where their meals are. Lale sees that the camp commandant is very old. Lale talks to approachable guards, and finds that he is mostly with Poles, Russians and Italians. As it appears that he is the only Slovakian there, Lale mostly keeps to himself, despite his facility with languages.

One day, Lale is approached by two young men who say that they've been told that he was the Tatowierer at Auschwitz. Neither of these men had been at Auschwitz themselves though. Perhaps foolishly, Lale says dismissively that he was the Tatowierer. It's not long after this that some SS officers grab

Lale and bring him before the camp commandant. Lale's tattooed identification number is revealed.

Lale admits that he was in Auschwitz, and that he was the Tatowierer, but that he is a Catholic, not a Jew. When asked for a third time, Lale says that he can prove it by beginning to undo his trousers (to show that he is not circumcised). His bravado pays off, as the aged commandant tells him to stop undressing. Lale is breathing heavily from the strain afterwards, for, of course, he is circumcised.

In one of the outer offices, he asks the date from one of the SS officers, and finds out that it's the 23rd of April 1945. So he has now been imprisoned by the Nazis for three years and resolves to make it not one day longer by escaping. It helps that the guards look very lazy. (This is remarkable, given that Vienna was taken by the Red Army on 13th of April 1945. While there may have been a narrative imperative for Heather Morris to show that Lale spent exactly three years in captivity, this unfortunately doesn't stack up with the historical dates. This is another inaccuracy that detractors will use against *The Tattooist of Auschwitz*.) Lale finds a weak spot in the camp fence (which is not electrified) and lifts it up without bothering to see if he's been spotted). He goes into the forest to escape being spotted by German patrols. Lale hears the sounds of battle as he goes deeper into the forest.

Lale hears the sound of running water, so he heads in that direction, not caring that this brings him closer to the sound of battle, as he plans to surrender to whichever army is attacking – the Russians or the Americans. When he comes to the waterway, he sees that it is a river (the Danube according to maps of Saurer Werke area). From the sound of the cannon fire, Lale believes that it is the Russians that are attacking. The water is far colder than he'd been expecting, and he becomes alarmed at being so close to the battle. He lets the current take him away from the battle, and manages to drag himself out when he has reached comparative safety, before passing out.

Chapter 27

When Lale awakes, the sun is shining and his clothes have dried a bit. He sees some Russian soldiers on a road that look relaxed, and surrenders to them. The Russians don't care and just walk past him. He walks in the opposite direction to them, as he doesn't want to get involved in any engagements with the Germans.

Eventually, a Russian Jeep (the Red Army did have Jeeps) pulls up alongside him and an officer asks him who he is. Lale says that he's a prisoner from Auschwitz, which the officer has never heard of. Lale finds it incredible that the place where millions of people suffered is unknown. Since Lale speaks perfect Russian, the officer asks what other languages Lale can speak. Unfortunately, while Lale's gift for languages helped him to survive in Auschwitz, here it turns out to be a hindrance, as the officer takes Lale back to his headquarters as he has a job for him. Headquarters turns out to be a luxurious requisitioned chalet on the top of a hill filled to the brim with expensive furniture, fittings and artwork – a million miles away from the living conditions that Lale has had to put up with for the past few years.

Lale is brought before a senior Red Army official, who is told that Lale speaks both Russian and German, and so could be useful when communicating with the locals. "I suspect he's a Jew, but I don't think that matters." The senior official orders that a guard be put on Lale so he doesn't escape, but also that he's washed and given better clothes.

The Russian officer takes Lale upstairs, and tells him to help himself to the clothes there (which belonged to the previous occupants). Tiffany lamps were quite popular handmade art nouveau lamps in Germany and Austria, and were produced by the studio of the American Louis Comfort Tiffany (from the same family that ran the famous department store).

Lale finds a suit that will be a good fit. Lale luxuriates in his first bath for three years. The owner of the clothes must have been thin, as they hang well on Lale's emaciated frame. Lale takes in the view of the magnificent gardens. Then Lale is joined by his minder and another soldier. The minder observes that the chalet is far more splendid than the HQ they had at the front. The minder introduces the soldier, Fredrich, who has instructions to shoot Lale if he tries to escape. Fredrich is very unfriendly. However, Lale won Baretski over, so it's quite possible he could do the same with Fredrich.

Then Lale learns the true nature of his value to the Russians: they want him to go into the village each day to procure women for them. They go down to the vault, in which Lale sees that money and jewellery are being stored. The minder says that they need eight to ten women each night, whose services will be paid for by the valuables in the vault. The minder tells him that the women will be taken back to their homes. Obviously, this is all very unsavoury, and Lale is put in the situation of having to do morally dubious things to women while he is at gunpoint.

As discussed previously, there was a lot of sexual violence against German women at the end of World War II. For instance, the anonymous author of *A Woman in Berlin* (1959) wrote of how she turned to a Russian officer to protect her from the gang rapes that she had previously suffered from the Red Army in the fall of Berlin:

> By no means could it be said that the major is raping me... Am I doing it for bacon, butter, sugar, candles, canned meat? To some extent I'm sure I am. In addition I like the major and the less he wants from me as a man, the more I like him as a person.

'Liberators' from other Allied forces also expected sexual favours in exchange for giving the traumatised and bombed out women of Berlin food. (Much of Berlin had been flattened by Allied bombing raids.)

Lale is given the choice of eating in the kitchen or in his room. It's made clear to him that the only room that he's allowed to enter above the first floor is the room that has been allocated to him.

Lale is given a lamb dish to eat. However, he can't enjoy this rich food, as Gita is not there to share it. He wonders if she has anything to eat at all... [And if she has to make the same stark choices that many other women have to make in occupied Europe to survive?] Lale can't get out of the habit of saving half of his food. He drinks most of a bottle of red wine, and falls asleep drunk. He's awoken by the sound of a breakfast tray being placed next to his bed and wonders if the chef has a key to his room, and if he even locked it. It seems that his new duties as pimp had not been required the previous evening (perhaps it had been too late, or he'd been allowed time to "settle in").

Fredrich comes in and asks if he's ready. (So the procurement of women looks to start first thing in the morning.) They go to the vault the first time, and Lale suggests that he takes more money and gems than he needs, as he doesn't know what the going rate is yet. This is agreed to by the accountant officer, as long as he brings the extra currency back.

Fredrich gets a jeep and they head into the village. They will obviously have a bigger truck to pick up the young women later on. They go to the main street, and Fredrich advises him that he can approach any young woman that is preferably pretty. Some of the women have been to the chalet before. Others may well throw things at him, and others may well have their own boyfriends. (This is all very 'genteel' compared to the horror stories of mass rapes by the Red Army. Presumably the officers were supposed to be less brutal in their procurement of women from the territories that they had conquered than the ordinary soldiers.)

Lale goes into a boutique, and is relieved to see that none of the women are joined by their husbands or boyfriends. (Surely their husbands or boyfriends would still be in the army, displaced across Europe? According to http://countrystudies.us/austria/41.htm, "some 800,000 Austrians were drafted into the army (the German Wehrmacht), and another 150,000 served in the Waffen SS" during World War II, and some of the most prominent Nazis (i.e. Hitler) were Austrian. Obviously, this little village wouldn't have been the target of mass bombing, but these women would likely have suffered some trauma during the war, especially since the German army vigorously resisted the Red Army's invasion of Eastern Austria. However, Austrian enthusiasm for the Nazi cause from the Anschluss in 1938 had cooled down considerably by 1945, and the Western Allies encountered comparatively little resistance as they made their way through western Austria.)

Since the stories of the Red Army raping their way through Europe are now regarded as historical fact, these women's acquiescence in their prostitution is surprising. Perhaps like *A Woman in Berlin*, they thought that giving sexual favours to Russian officers would stop them from being gang raped. On the other hand, it could be that these women were making pragmatic decisions, due to their uncertain futures at the end of the war. Hard cash and jewellery might well go a long way in feeding them and their families. As we have seen from Auschwitz, the prisoners there had to make many unethical judgement calls in their bid to survive, that they would never had have to make in peacetime. Making the decision to fraternise with the enemy was also quite risky: women accused of "collaboration horizontale" following the liberation of France had their heads shaved in punishment, and some were murdered. As Anthony Beevor wrote in his 2009 article "An Ugly Carnival" in *The Guardian*:

> Many victims were young mothers, whose husbands were in German prisoner-of-war camps. During the war, they often had no means of support, and their only hope of obtaining food for themselves and their children was to accept a liaison with a German

soldier.... Jealousy masqueraded as moral outrage, because people envied the food and entertainment these women had received as a result of their conduct.

(https://www.theguardian.com/lifeandstyle/2009/jun/05/women-victims-d-day-landings-second-world-war)

So these women received a patriarchal punishment for doing what they needed to do to survive during a war manufactured by patriarchs. Beevor believes that some of these women were accused by men as a means of deflecting attention away from their own collaboration with the enemy. This is probably the kind of punishment that we will see meted out to Cilka in Heather Morris's follow up to *The Tattooist of Auschwitz*.

Although this scene seems surprising given the context of the Red Army's well-known rapes, it must be true, as the officers wouldn't have needed Lale if their intention was to just rape these women – as they could have just done that at gunpoint. This is another invaluable aspect to Lale's eyewitness testimony, as he was in a relatively unique position here to report that the Red Army's sexual relations with women in the lands that they had conquered could be more nuanced than just descending to brutal rape.

Lale is rather relieved when one of the shop assistants speaks up and makes things easier for him, by asking if he's been sent to find out if they want to "party" in the chalet. Lale is obviously embarrassed by his task, but the women make him feel more at ease as he goes about his business. The shop assistant who first spoke makes it clear why they are engaging with him:

"We all know what you want, and there are plenty of us who need good food and drink even if we have to share it with those ugly Russian pigs. There are no men left here to help us. We do what we have to do."

So it looks like the women will be given food and drink, as well as being paid for attending the "party". Lale successfully completes negotiations with the required number of women.

Later that evening, Lale and Fredrich pick up the women, and Lale pays them the remainder of the money as agreed. The women are resolute as they enter the chalet. Fredrich then demands that Lale gives him the left over money, and pats him down to make sure that Lale hasn't pocketed any. Lale jokes about not knowing Fredrich well enough to let him be so intimate with him. Hopefully the Russian accountant has a full record of the jewels and cash in the safe, as Lale could get into trouble if he still has the two diamonds left over from Auschwitz.

Lale's dinner is brought up to him, and he is relieved to only hear laughter and conversation drifting up from below. Lale reveals that he has a diamond stuffed away in the cuff of his trousers, which he must have risked stealing from the Russians.

He wakes up from a sleep to hear the sound of the women being taken back in the truck, and is relieved to see that none look distressed.

These twice daily trips to the village become Lale's routine. He always goes to the boutique and the café, where he is warmly greeted. Lale's love of women helps him in his task, as he's often asked if he's going to join the party that night, and the women seem genuinely disappointed when he says that he cannot. One of the waitresses in the café, Serena, outright asks him if he will marry her when the war is over, and she is quite indignant when Lale tells her that his heart belongs to someone else. He tells the women about Gita, and about how he's sure that she's still alive somewhere, although he doesn't know where she is.

Lale keeps smuggling gems over the weeks; hiding gems upon his person is something that he became accustomed to during his time at Auschwitz. However, one night he is surprised by a knock on the door as he's counting the gems, and doesn't notice a ruby falling on the floor. Fredrich asks why the door was locked, and Lale says that he doesn't want to be propositioned to by one of the gay officers. Fredrich observes that such officers would pay him well if he offered such services. Fredrich then offers one of the women from the village to him, but then notices the ruby glittering on the floor.

Lale quickly suggests that the ruby must have got caught in the lining of his clothes. Fredrich seems satisfied with Lale's explanation and takes the ruby back to the vault. Before he does so, he tells Lale that he's being transferred, so Lale will be doing the trips to the village by himself from now on, as he has shown that he can be trusted. Fredrich says the general may even give Lale a bonus once the Russians have finished there. Lale tells Fredrich to look after himself, as there's still a war on; although, there is not much of a war in Europe left, as Germany unconditionally surrendered on the 8th of May 1945.

It's obvious by the way that Lale is preparing his clothes that night that he is going to leave with his stolen booty at the very first opportunity the next day. (Obviously the Russians had stolen the cash and jewellery themselves anyway.)

110

Lale goes to the vault as usual, but is stopped by the accountant on the way out. Fortunately, the accountant just wants to give him extra cash and jewels, as they will have to entertain two senior officers from Moscow that evening. Lale tells the accountant that he might be a bit late, as he wants to borrow a book from the village library. The accountant points out that they have a good library in the chalet, but Lale says he's a bit worried about going in there, as there are always scary looking officers in there.

Lale drives the jeep into the village, and then abandons it. While it's a fast form of transport, he wouldn't get far in a Russian army jeep. Sure enough, he's soon stopped by a Russian army patrol after he's stolen a bike from the village. One of the soldiers takes the bike away from him, so he's forced to continue on foot.

As evening falls, he approaches a town that is full of Russian soldiers, so he decides to avoid the centre. He finds the train station, which has a train waiting. Lale is understandably wary of the train, due to his previous experiences on cattle trucks, but this train is most definitely one for people.

Lale approaches the stationmaster and finds out (to his delight) that the train is headed for Bratislava. Lale pays for the journey by giving the station master two diamonds. As he pays, his sleeve rides up, showing his tattoo. The stationmaster advises him to get in the end carriage, as no one will disturb him there. The train is not going to leave for another eight hours though.

As he goes to get on the end carriage, the stationmaster shouts out to him, and kindly gives Lale some food and drink that his wife made for him. Lale is brought to tears by this act of kindness from a stranger who has taken pity on him. It would appear that news of the atrocities carried out at Auschwitz have reached the wider world.

Day breaks as the train enters Slovakia. A train guard asks Lale for his papers, and Lale simply replies by showing his tattoo and saying that he is Slovakian. The train guard welcomes Lale home.

Chapter 28

Lale gets off the train in Bratislava, the city he should have lived in for the last three years. Many of the streets are barely recognisable due to bombing. Unaware that Gita is in the city, Lale believes that there is nothing for him there, and resolves to go back to his family home at Krompachy. It is something that he would have had to do, sooner rather than later; although he's likely to face grim news when he arrives, such is the mass murder that the Nazis carried out against the Jews. Krompachy is 250 miles away, and Lale walks for part of the journey, and fortunately gets rides along the way. But such is his rapid progress that he doesn't appear to rest much. He pays for his journey using the purloined jewels.

Eventually he arrives outside his family home, which is rundown and deserted. He's confronted by an elderly woman from across the street, who turns out to be one of his neighbours, Mrs Molnar.

Some of the Auschwitz inmates had very unpleasant experiences when they returned home. Laurence Rees reports the account of Linda Breder's return to her Slovakian home:

> She wandered off down the main street of her home town, and as she did so the sudden realization came to her that all the houses that had previously belonged to her friends and relations were now occupied by people from the Soviet Union... Only the non-Jewish population of the town were still in evidence, but many of them had previously been friendly with Linda and her family and she thought they at least would welcome her. She was wrong... "Everyone kept their distance as if I was poisoned or something... Going back was my worst experience."

(*Auschwitz: the Nazis and the 'Final Solution'*, 2005)

Mrs Molnar finally recognizes Lale and they embrace. The woman appears to have aged beyond her years. Mrs Molnar is finally able to tell Lale that his sister, Goldie, is still living in the family home.

Without any further ado, Lale crosses the street and knocks on the door, which Goldie finally opens. She faints when she sees her long-lost brother. Mrs Molnar joins him and helps him take Goldie to the sofa. Goldie recovers, and tells Lale the bad news: his parents were taken away just days after he left, and his brother Max was killed fighting the Nazis as a partisan. Max's two boys and his wife were taken away. However, Goldie has married a

Russian called Sokolov, who is away on business. In the "Additional Information" section at the end of the book, Heather Morris reveals that Lale's parents were taken to Auschwitz on 26th March 1942, and that they were executed upon arrival as part of the 'Final Solution'. From the very beginning of his Auschwitz torment, one of the things that kept Lale going was the belief that his family would be safe back home. It must have been devastating for him to hear that his beloved mother had been taken away just days after he had left home. Heather Morris relates that Lale never knew that his mother and father were murdered at Auschwitz even before he arrived there.

Lale only tells Goldie that he's been in a Polish work camp without wanting to go into all the details. But he does tell Goldie and Mrs Molnar all about Gita. They tell him that he must look for her, but then comes the crux: Gita never told him where she came from during their three years together in Auschwitz, and that all he knows is her surname. (But we know that Gita is registered with the Red Cross, so this may be all that Lale needs.)

Mrs Molnar tells Lale that all the people from the camps are heading to Bratislava (where he's just been, of course). Lale needs transport, but doesn't find anyone in the village that can help him. Finally he stops a man with a horse and cart, and offers to buy them with some jewels. The man agrees, as long as Lale takes him home first. Then Lale goes back to his family home with the horse and cart.

That night, Goldie and Mrs Molnar make him meals for his journey. Lale is sorry to be leaving so soon, but Goldie understands that he must find Gita.

Lale travels for three days and nights, and gives other people lifts along the way. (Of course, he would know his way around a horse and cart thanks to his father's taxi business. Although this sounds like a very arduous journey for the horse – it must have taken more than three days the travel the 250 miles back to Bratislava.)

When he arrives in Bratislava, he goes immediately to the rail station, and asks if it's true that refugees from the camps have been turning up there. He decides to meet every arriving train. He doesn't think any lodging houses would take both him and the horse, so he decides to live off the cart as his friends the Romany would have done. It's coming to the end of summer, and the weather is getting colder.

After weeks of asking new arrivals about Gita, the stationmaster finally tells Lale that he would be better off checking with the Red Cross.

Gita finally comes across the young man and his cart in the main street. Time stands still as they finally meet, and Lale seems unable to move. Gita confirms that it is Lale to one of her friends. Gita tells Lale that the final thing she said to him as she was forced out of Auschwitz was: "I love you". Lale asks her to marry him, and Gita says yes. Lale is finally able to embrace and kiss her, and the young couple walk off together into the war ravaged streets.

Epilogue

Heather Morris relates that Lale adopted the surname of his sister's husband, Sokolov, as this name was more acceptable in the Soviet post-war rule of Slovakia. "Sokolov" is the name from a town in the east of the Czech Republic, which is possibly where the surname derives; possibly Lale thought that Eisenberg sounded too Jewish, and if that's the case, then obviously he still feared anti-Semitism under Russian rule. Having written that, Eisenberg means "Iron Mountain", which would be a fitting name for life under the "Iron Curtain". However, the most likely reason why Lale changes his name is that he does not want to be recognised as the Tattooist of Auschwitz, and accused of collaborating with the Nazis. (This is probably why Lale and Gita didn't travel to the new state of Israel, despite sending funds to help the new state.) After all, many of the SS adopted new names and went into hiding to avoid being sentenced for death for war crimes. Mengele notoriously escaped to Argentina.

Of course, as Heather Morris relates, one SS man who did not escape was Commandant Rudolf Höss, who was executed at the site of his mass murders on 16th April 1947.

Höss on the gallows at Auschwitz. (Public domain image)

Lale and Gita married soon after the war, in October 1945.

While I have pointed out many errors in *The Tattooist of Auschwitz*, I am very supportive of all the hard work that Heather Morris put into telling Lale's story. As I have previously written, it's impossible to write such a long book without making errors. Mistakes are also inevitable when dealing

115

with such testimonies, as eye witnesses can make mistakes reporting incidents that they saw 5 minutes ago, let alone 50 decades previously. I don't think these factual errors, or the dramatic licence that Heather Morris uses, get in the way of Lale's story at all. There is no dispute that Lale was a Tattooist at Auschwitz. Professional historians have to evaluate eye witness testimony all the time, and debate the accuracy of events, and the biases of the particular author. In my consideration, Lale's testimony provides evidence that has not been recorded before, and so *The Tattooist of Auschwitz*, despite being presented as a novel, is also an important historical document. Although it would be better if Heather Morris's publishers are more scrupulous in their fact checking for *Cilka's Journey*, as the sequel may possibly be scrutinised by millions of readers.

Made in the USA
Middletown, DE
04 August 2019